CIVIL SERVICE DEPARTMENT

Civil Service College Studies

1

New Trends
in Government

Lectures delivered by
Sir Richard Clarke K.C.B., O.B.E.
at the Civil Service College
between March 1 and April 5, 1971

LONDON
HER MAJESTY'S STATIONERY OFFICE
1971

First published 1971
Second impression 1972

SBN 11 630264 X

ii

CONTENTS

FOREWORD

By Sir William Armstrong, G.C.B., C.V.O.

One consequence of the October, 1970 changes in the machinery of government was that Sir Richard Clarke, formerly Permanent Secretary of the Ministry of Technology, became available for special duties for a short period before his retirement from the public service on the age-limit.

The six lectures published in this book were prepared in this period. They were given in March and April 1971 under the auspices of the Civil Service College to an audience of senior civil servants and other public sector and academic representatives. The lectures were followed by a weekend seminar at the College in which over 40 of those who attended the lectures took part.

The lectures are published here in the form in which they were given, with a postscript by Sir Richard setting out his further thoughts on these matters following the discussions at the seminar. I need hardly add that Sir Richard chose the subjects of the lectures himself, and the opinions which he expresses are his own.

The purpose of the lectures and the seminar was to fund the experience of a Permanent Secretary of eight years' standing in the Treasury and in the Ministries of Aviation and Technology, who had been very closely involved in the new trends of government which are the subject of the lectures ; to contribute to professional thought and discussion on these very critical and important questions ; and to help and inform the work of the Civil Service Department including the Civil Service College. In my opinion, shared by others who took part, the undertaking made a valuable contribution on all these scores ; and I hope that it will be equally useful to the wider audience to which it is now presented.

FOREWORD

by Sir William Armstrong G.C.B.

Introduction

It is a remarkable privilege at the end of my civil service career to be allowed to talk for six hours to whoever of my colleagues cares to listen. It is a great pleasure to be able to do it under the auspices of the Civil Service College ; and I am deeply grateful to Sir William Armstrong and Mr Grebenik for making this possible. I hope the lectures will be valuable, both as a funding of experience and as an exercise in speculation about the future ; and that in published form they will be of some use to the training programmes of the College.

I decided to devote these lectures to public administration and not to policy ; partly because it is easier for even a retiring civil servant to talk about administration ; but even more because we are entering into a highly interesting period in administration, with the new 'giant' departments and the new concepts of Programme Analysis Review (PAR) ; and it so happens that for the last ten years I have been heavily engaged in these matters, both as Head of the Public Sector Group at the Treasury, and as Permanent Secretary first of the Ministry of Aviation and then of a succession of three Ministries of Technology each much bigger than the last, and then itself divided and merged between others.

I have had most helpful comments from colleagues ; but I hasten to say that these lectures are all my own work and contain nothing, I trust, that contravenes the Official Secrets Acts ; that they fly no kites for any Minister or for anyone else ; and that I alone am responsible for them. But I shall not be trying to awaken reforming zeal. The view of the former Permanent Secretary of the Ministry of Technology is bound to be that 'enough change is enough'. What I shall try to do is to discuss on a strictly professional basis the implications of the changes of machinery of government that have been taking place (both in the previous and in the present administrations) ; and see where this might lead us by the middle 1970s ; and identify which are the points to watch and which are the developments to think about. My object is to begin to suggest a sort of navigation chart for the administrator of the 1970s.

There are six lectures. The first two are about the 'giant' departments : then there are two about the organisation at the centre of Whitehall, and the relation between the centre and the departments ; then one on the relations between the State and public corporations—concentrating first on nationalised industries. and then on 'hiving off' and the like : the final one in two parts, one on scientific research ; the last drawing the conclusions for the civil service. I am afraid there are a lot of subjects left untouched. But that shows how big the subject is ; and six lectures are quite enough.

NEW TRENDS IN GOVERNMENT

1 'Giant' Departments

One characteristic of the next period in machinery of government is the emergence of the 'giant' departments, unprecedentedly large in breadth of business and with large staffs and scale of operation. They are unitary departments, with one Cabinet Minister in charge, with the full statutory powers and responsibility to Parliament ; and one Permanent Secretary responsible to him.

This is a different concept from that of an 'overlord' Minister over two or more Ministers, introduced in the 1951 Conservative Government and abandoned because of the clash between the 'overlord's' responsibility for the Ministers' work and their responsibility to Parliament. The idea was tried again as a temporary expedient in the October 1969 reorganisation, in which Mr Crosland was given certain 'overlord' responsibilities over the Ministers of Housing and Local Goverment and Transport ; but it would not have survived.

The 'giant' department is a different concept also from that of a 'federal' department, composed of a number of self-contained depart-ments and sub-departments, each with its powers and responsbilities, but with a Minister in charge with specified responsibilities and a super-structure of organisation to enable him to carry these out. The disadvantage of the 'federal' system is that it tends to perpetuate differences between the federated elements, instead of leading towards an effective combination. It is a different concept also from that of joining a number of separate but related departments under one Minister, e.g. the Treasury, Inland Revenue and Customs & Excise under the Chancellor of the Exchequer.

The 'giant' department is constitutionally just like any other department, but much bigger. It is likely to have at least another Minister, in addition to its head, of status equivalent to that of a Minister in charge of a department not represented in the Cabinet (i.e. an £8,500 per year Minister) : it will have one or more Second Permanent Secretaries (men of Permanent Secretary rank just one notch below the Permanent Secretary). The characteristic is of scale of business and organisation, and not of constitutional practice.

The 'Giant' Departments

There are now five Departments that I would put in this category. The Foreign and Commonwealth Office (FCO) which may be taken as including the old Ministry of Overseas Development though the association is 'federal' rather than unitary and the Ministry of Defence are very large, with particularly coherent functions and fields of operation. The Department of Trade and Industry (DTI) and the Department of the Environment (DOE) are the two new 'giants', both of great size and breadth of activity. The Department of Health and Social Security (DHSS) may be regarded as a 'giant', primarily on grounds of numbers and spend. *

The distinction is seen most clearly when we compare these with the next group in size—Home Office, Department of Education and Science (DES), Department of Employment (DE), Ministry of Agriculture, Fisheries and Food (MAFF), Scottish Office, and, at the time of this lecture, Ministry of Aviation Supply (MAS). These are large departments, but all unquestionably within the scope of one Minister of Cabinet rank and one Permanent Secretary on conventional lines. Nevertheless, some of what is said below about the 'giants' applies also to them.

I must add that the Ministry of Technology became a 'giant' ('second Mintech') on its merger with the Ministry of Aviation in February 1967, and a large one ('last Mintech') when merged with the Ministry of Power and much of the Board of Trade and DEA in October 1969. I was Permanent Secretary throughout these proceedings, and much of what is said here follows our experiences both of commission and omission, and is designed to extract the lessons from this experience.

The tables in Annex 1 set out the arithmetic for all these departments, together with the Treasury, Civil Service Department, and Cabinet Office.

'Giants' : Pros and Cons

It has been said that the merging into 'giant' departments is in some way

* Note that the first two of these have been developing, stage by stage, for many years ; that the last was created by the previous administration ; that the 'giant' DTI replaced the 'giant' Mintech ; and that the post-election statements by the previous administration favour DOE ; so the approach to 'giant' departments has certainly been an all-party one.

analogous to mergers between industrial firms, part of the move to 'bigness'. This is too facile. The analogous unit to an industrial firm— immensely larger and more complicated, of course—is the operation of government as a whole, for this is what has (or should have) one central purpose and one direction. The appearance of a 'giant' department does not represent an increase in the size of the 'firm' (as one may put it) of government : it simply reflects the thought that it is more efficient to operate with ten large departments rather than with over 20 small ones. The analogy with industry if there is one is really with a holding company deciding to concentrate its interests into a smaller number of units, in order to get more effective operating units and a better communication with the centre.

The advantages which are hoped for are set out in last October's White Paper, *The Reorganisation of Central Government.*[1] In essence, they are four. The 'giant' can develop its own strategy and decide its own priorities ; it can settle problems itself instead of lengthy discussion in interdepartmental committees ; it is big enough to have specialised services ; it can support a clearer strategy at the centre. These are important advantages if they can be secured ; and my experience in Mintech was that we could reasonably hope to achieve them in time. But the time-scale is as relevant in govermental organisation as in industry ; and it takes years to get benefit from such changes.

The potential disadvantages are also important. The biggest danger is that of excessive pressure on the Ministers ; and linked with this is the danger of muddle and conflict between the Ministers, and therefore delay in the business. The five or six Ministers in the 'giant' must work as a team together ; and this requires good temperaments and good organisation. Likewise it is early to say with assurance that the 'giant' can be managed at the official level in a manner which brings clear policy determination and rapid execution : there is no reason to argue that this cannot be done, but the scale is unprecedentedly great. Lastly, there is always danger in government that favourable changes are made but the advantages are not realised because of the inertia of the system—you get benefits from doing something new, but are required at the same time to continue the old, and thus make no net savings at all.

The Ministerial Operation

For Ministerial operation, the limiting factor on the size of the 'giant' is the amount of the department's business that must go to Cabinet and the Minister's ability to absorb and handle it. However effectively the Minister devolves the work on to his junior colleagues, the load of

[1] Cmnd 4506, para 12.

departmental Cabinet business is inescapable. If it stops the Cabinet Minister from doing the rest of his Cabinet and political work, his contact with Parliament, and his activities outside, the system becomes unmanageable.

There is no sure way round this difficulty. There have been many cases of having two Cabinet Ministers in one department. Often in the last ten years both the Chancellor of the Exchequer and the Chief Secretary of the Treasury (in charge of public expenditure) were in the Cabinet: sometimes, as now, two Foreign Office Ministers: and Mr Benn and Mr Lever were both Cabinet Ministers in 'last Mintech'. But this is inconsistent with the idea of a small Cabinet; and it is difficult to justify the concept of a 'giant' department with more work of national and political importance to the Cabinet than its Minister can comprehend and handle. The same argument refutes the idea of allowing the No 2 Minister to attend the Cabinet for particular business. If the Cabinet business cannot be handled effectively by the one Cabinet Minister, the department is too big.

On the other hand, the Minister's load can be greatly eased if the fields of responsibility of his No 2's are clearly enough defined to enable the No 2's to be accepted by Parliament as the spokesmen in all but the most critical occasions (which the Minister will be handling in Cabinet anyway); and it is important too that the outside interests involved in the department's work (industry, local government etc) shall be content to see the No 2 and not insist on seeing the Minister. There is enough experience so far to suggest that this can be achieved, provided that it is known that the Minister will always back up the No. 2.

In my judgment, this is the area of greatest potential difficulty; for there are important human problems and questions of the reaction of other institutions and outside individuals to them. The ability to run his team of departmental Ministers, some only just below him in rank and party standing, and some only just up from the back benches, is thus becoming one of the main qualifications for a Cabinet Minister in charge of a 'giant' department. Formerly, with one or two junior ministers, the Minister would give them specific tasks which he thought appropriate to their capability and let them get on with them, handling the important issues himself. But now the success of the team, which will include three or sometimes even more levels of Minister, is fundamental; and the Minister will be wise to provide time for regular formal meetings with all of them, and for informal discussions too. If they try to act as individual Ministers in charge of sub-departments, or even if only one gets out of step with the others, there can be heavy cost to the department's work and to the Minister's position. In my personal experience, I would say that these problems can be dealt with satisfactorily; but it is easy to underestimate their importance and difficulty.

4

Departmental Organisation

Strong organisation of the department is a necessary condition, though not always a sufficient one, for the success of the ministerial operation. In the 'giant' department with its greater numbers of ministers and senior officials and greater intricacy of organisation and working methods, the possibility of tension and confusion is not necessarily worse than can occur in a smaller department with a single Minister and a single Permanent Secretary. But it is a hazard which is always there; and the bigger the department, the more at stake.

With a Permanent Secretary and two Second Permanent Secretaries, it will normally be sensible to divide the whole into three—two large 'wings' of the department under the two Second Permanent Secretaries, and a central area in the middle under Deputy Secretaries comprising the establishment and management services, allocation of resources and finance, and the central policy common to the whole department. The chart in Annex 2 shows how this was done in 'last Mintech'; and the initial structure of DTI is not dissimilar. The ease or otherwise with which this is done depends greatly upon the subject-matter: in 'last Mintech' it was perhaps easier than in the present 'giant' departments because the aviation side could have a considerable autonomy in day-to-day operations without prejudicing its links with the rest of the department in industrial policy, economic appraisal, research.

It is not in my view wise, however, to make these wings more 'self-sufficient' than the nature of the work requires. The 'giant' departments are created to bring functions together, and the articulation across the department is just as important as the command structure up and down. The divisions in the central area are under the Permanent Secretary, but they serve the whole department; and it is important to avoid the building of as it were competing 'general policy' divisions in the 'wings'.

Indeed, in my opinion there is much to be said for distributing the responsibility between junior ministers in a different pattern from that of the departmental structure. They must have firm bailiwicks: but if they each have a hierarchical structure below them, like a sub-department, this does not help the objective of bringing the aspects of the department's work together.

The Permanent Secretary's role is bound to become different from that in a conventional department. He is, of course, still the adviser and confidant of the Minister on the most important issues; and notably about the objectives and strategies of the department. But his time will be heavily occupied with the higher management of the department—organisation, allocation of financial and other resources, personnel, relations with the Treasury and the Civil Service Department, and a fair amount of representational work outside. He will be unwise to try to play an active part over a wide field of the policy work of the department, which in this kind of department must be the province of the Second Permanent Secretaries and the Deputy Secretaries. Different Permanent Secretaries have different interests and styles of work ; but in my experience the management work (taken in its widest sense) is bound to occupy a very large part of his time.

Establishment & Budget Committee

The instrument which was used in both 'second' and 'last Mintech' for the higher management of the department was a committee which was called the Establishment & Budget Committee which contained all the people at HQ of Deputy Secretary or equivalent rank and above (of whom there were 15 in 'last Mintech') together with the heads of the Establishment & Management Services and Finance & Economic Appraisal Divisions.

This was somewhat unwieldy[2] but it had the advantages of making all the top echelon participate in the management work and of assuring every member of the staff that his or her interests were represented in the place in the department responsible for the promotion boards, appointments, office arrangements, discipline etc. The psychological advantages were important in a department brought together by a succession of mergers and containing a wide variety of administrative, scientific, engineer, statistician, executive etc staff. For considering the department's policy on the civil service issues in the Fulton Report, we had a special sub-committee which again tried to represent as wide a cross-section of the Department's staff as we could.

The most important central task of the department is to determine the objective and the strategy for reaching them, and the allocation of resources and deployment of staff for this purpose. One side of the task is the creation of the instrument—so to speak the 'establishment' side of the work : the other is the way in which the instrument is used— so to speak, the 'budget' side of the work. These two functions are inextricably mixed together : and it was the idea of bringing the whole of the top echelon into this dual process that led to the Establishment & Budget Committee.

In both 'second' and 'last Mintech' we were all too occupied with the actual problems of carrying out the successive mergers to formulate this as lucidly as we should have done. Again, in 'last Mintech' the size of the committee was too great, so we divided up into two panels, one for 'establishment' and one for 'budget' : on the principles above this may well have been the wrong course, and we should have gone for a smaller Executive covering the whole field, while retaining the wider body covering the whole top echelon, for those occasions in which it was thought necessary to get advice across the whole department and

[2] The title also ; it should have been *'Management Committee'*.

to be seen to be doing so. However this may be done, there seem to me advantages (both in 'giant' departments and in those of more conventional size) in handling this essential central work together, and in finding means of representing the whole of the department in the process.

Objectives and Resource Allocation

The emphasis now being placed on the formulation of objectives, review of how they are being carried out, and the allocation of resources to do it is relatively new in departments. The Plowden Report on the Control of Public Expenditure[3] was the first stage. Its main preoccupation, however, was to relate public expenditure programmes and decision-making more effectively with consideration of the prospective national economic resources likely to be available when the expenditure took place. The impact in Whitehall was therefore largely in terms of allocation of resources between departments; and the Public Expenditure Survey Committee (PESC) apparatus became set up for this purpose rather than for getting clearer departmental objectives and priorities within them. The emphasis became focussed less upon the examination of what each department was proposing to do than upon the division of resources between them.

The new Programme Analysis Review (PAR) foreshadowed in paras 51 and 52 of Cmnd 4506 is meant to improve the balance, providing for submission by departments of statements of objectives and statements of priorities for central consideration before the process of allocation begins. PAR will be even more important to 'giant' departments' own operations than to the interdepartmental allocation operation.

Departments will have to organise themselves to produce their PARs as well as their PESCs; and the natural expectation would be to do this in one central division, which would of course come under the Permanent Secretary. The reviews would be approved in the department for the Minister's decision by some such process as was provided by the 'last Mintech' Establishment & Budget Committee. It would seem natural for this division generally to do the conventional finance work also, for the preparation of the PAR and PESC returns and the translation of the Cabinet's decisions on the PESC allocation into terms of departmental action is difficult to separate from the traditional estimates and accounting functions.

[3] Cmnd 2432 of July 1961. For the successive stages in the development of the PESC system, see Cmnd 2235 of Dec. 1963, Cmnd 2915 of February 1966, Cmnd 3515 of Jan. 1968, Cmnd 3936 of February 1969, Cmnd 4017 of April 1969, Cmnd 4234 of Dec. 1969, and Cmnd 4578 of Jan. 1971, described in Sir Samuel Goldman's lecture on 'The Presentation of Public Expenditure Proposals to Parliament' in the Autumn 1970 issue of *Public Administration*.

Management of Finance

In a large department, however, to attempt to centralise the financial business must be inefficient. If there are more than, say, 25 units in a department which are spending money, the attempt to filter all their dealings with the Treasury through a Finance Division will lead to great delay. It is essential to proper management that the people who are spending the money should carry the full responsibility for the way in which the money is spent, and should not be able to push this responsibility on to a Finance Division. So a large department must have a decentralised system of financial control and administration.

With this, however, must be combined a centralised system for deciding what expenditure should be undertaken. This will naturally be done by the division which deals with PAR and PESC, and here is the link with the more conventional work of handling estimates and accounts, conducting the departmental work with the Treasury and with Exchequer and Audit, and giving financial advice to the divisions. In more 'federally' organised departments, it is possible to split these functions; but in Mintech it always seemed simplest to run the PESC and the decision-making work together with the conventional Finance Division work; and I think this has much to commend it.

In 'last Mintech', where the civil tasks of the department included an immense variety of expenditures in industry—investment grants, local employment grants in the development areas, advisory services for industry, investment programmes of nationalised industries, launching aid for aircraft and aero-engine projects, support for shipbuilding and computer industries, IRC and NRDC, the financing of the Atomic Energy Authority, development contracts in industry, subsidies for industrial research associations, systems to establish standards and quality assurance, and the running of our own research establishments— the task was to develop an apparatus of economic appraisal which would enable us to judge whether we were using consistent criteria for expenditure decisions in all parts of the department, and of whether we were getting value for money under each head. So the department had a powerful multi-disciplined, Finance and Economic Appraisal Division, with two Under-Secretaries, to cover the entire range of questions.

A balance must be kept between the advantages of centralisation and those of decentralisation. As we have seen, it would be absurd to try to funnel the whole of a 'giant' department's financial transactions and business with the Treasury through one central division, both because of the delay that it would cause and because of the damaging effect on the financial responsibility of operating divisions. Likewise in economic appraisal, the work should be done in the operating divisions on principles and methods endorsed by the centre. So in Mintech we had a separate R & D Programmes Analysis Unit, jointly run by the department and

8

the Atomic Energy Authority, located at Harwell, with the original purpose of developing new techniques in this very difficult field. The bulk of the highly sophisticated economic evaluation of civil aircraft projects, now as sophisticated as the technical evaluation, was done in the Aviation Group. The economic appraisal of nationalised industry investment likewise was done in the divisions dealing with nationalised industry.

The objective should always be to have the centre strong enough to do the jobs that must be done in the centre—the appraisals and comparisons that have to be made across the whole department, and the determination and advice on the methods to be adopted and the parameters to be used throughout the department—but not stronger than that, or the operating parts of the department will be weakened and their responsibility undermined. This question of balance is fundamental: if a choice has to be made it is better to be too weak in the centre than too strong.

The same consideration applies to economics and statistics. In order to use economic advice and statistics in the most effective way, it is highly desirable for the economists and statisticians to work as closely as possible with the operating divisions ; with only enough in the centre to do the tasks which must be done there, and to provide the necessary amount of professional leadership and co-ordination throughout the department.

'Planning Units'

The development of PAR and PESC, and the idea of the central unit in the 'giant' department to deal with them also brings into perspective the concept of 'planning units' set out in the Fulton Report. The Fulton Committee thought that departments were so occupied with day-to-day business that they could not consider long-term policy, and advised that there should be 'planning units', outside the normal stream of departmental organisation, for the purpose. The PAR system deals with this by providing an annual requirement to state the department's objectives and priorities which generally meets this point.

There is, however, a further point of whether a department is taking enough account of the periods further ahead than is involved in its normal decision-making. In 'last Mintech' the normal time-scale of the department's day-to-day work was about ten years ahead. The decisions on civil aircraft projects, authorisation of construction of power stations, nuclear R & D, programmes of research establishments all depend on the national economy about ten years ahead, i.e. in the early 1980s. There seemed to be advantage in considering a situation somewhat further away, say in the late 1980s, to see whether we could discern any trends that we should be taking into account so far ahead. This is highly speculative, but well worth considering, for one is always at risk of implicitly relying on projections of existing trends, which will usually turn out wrong. In Mintech we kept in touch with developments in the new industry of technological forecasting; but we never actually set up our 'very long-term' unit, for we never succeeded in finding the man—scientist or economist or administrator—with the special qualities of mind needed to do this kind of forward-looking work with feet firmly planted on the ground.

The need varies between departments, largely according to the time-scale of their day-to-day work. In some cases, the need may be for a unit which could examine specific long-term policy questions outside the normal run of the divisions' work—a unit changing in composition according to the task to be done. All this fits well into a division or divisions which does the PAR/PESC work.

The 'Budget' Division

The combination of PAR and PESC, and the need for more intensive appraisal of expenditures and for 'planning units' etc. have created a different role for finance from what was the position even ten years ago. The old 'finance' function epitomised by the proper cash accounting for expenditure was superseded long ago, and the Permanent Secretary's role as Accounting Officer has widened far beyond his responsibility to account before the Public Accounts Committee (PAC) for inefficiencies and improprieties committed by his department. But we have only recently reached the stage at which we could formulate the central financial resource planning and allocation role, and add it to the old financial control role. I would call this division the 'Budget' Division, and let the time-honoured Finance Division title disappear for a few years until the new systems are firmly established. In a 'giant' department, titles are important; for the words help people to understand how to think about their work.

Parliamentary Control

The examination by Exchequer and Audit and the nature of the proceedings of the Public Accounts Committee have been changing at the same time; but the implications for the Exchequer and Audit system of the new role of finance have not yet fully appeared. There must always be parliamentary control of departmental expenditure; for this is valuable both for Parliament and for the departments. But it is important that the control should bite upon the right points, and that it should have a constructive effect on departments' work, and not lead to expenditure of time and effort chasing after the wrong things.

For Parliament to exert the greatest possible pressure upon the efficiency of the departments' financial management and control, changes would be needed in the present Supply and audit procedures. Their historic

10

purpose was to ensure that the moneys voted by Parliament were used
for the purposes intended by Parliament (and *inter alia* did not vanish
into the pockets of Ministers and officials). Successive Comptroller-
and-Auditors-General have tried to work them as constructively as
they can. But when the government handles public expenditure by a
PESC allocation system, with emphasis on the determination of each
department's aggregate spending and the way in which decisions are
taken about this spending, whilst parliamentary Supply procedures
follow the traditional concept of public expenditure consisting of
hundreds of thousands of individual items controlled item by item, then
the process of parliamentary control is bound to become remote from
the real work.

It would be interesting indeed to add up the time spent on Supply
procedure by departments and Parliament year by year, and to know
what cases there have been in the past ten years in which the work
of a department has been done better and more sensibly as a result
of these procedures, or in which Parliament has been able to exercise a
genuine constraint on the government by virtue of them. How many
of Exchequer and Audit's referrals to departments likewise have resulted
in better understanding by the department of its problems and consequent
action to improve its efficiency?

I would myself like to see a great simplification of procedure, with the
number of Votes reduced from the present 166 to about 20—one for
each important department and the minor departments brought
together into one Treasury Vote; and the whole paraphernalia of
sub-heads, virement, special treatment of grants-in-aid, control of
write-offs etc. drastically reduced. It is sometimes said that these
procedures are harmless. But they use staff and they use time, and
sometimes quite a lot of both, and they tend to create an idea that
finance is a formal ritual and not the centre of policy. One wonders,
indeed, whether anything more is required than the voting of the money
in the simplest possible way, department by department, in terms which
put total responsibility on the departmental Minister and his Permanent
Secretary, and then the audit and approval of the accounts of how the
money has been spent. Certainly to my mind the onus of proof should
be on those who claim that any greater control should be retained.

The question of control is different from that of the amount of information
given in the Estimates and the Appropriation Account. In the simplification operation of the early 1960s, designed to give as clear a picture as
possible of each department's spending and manpower, the detail was
reduced sufficiently to include all the Estimates within one volume of
850 pages; which is probably about right. Alas, the Civil Department's
Estimates now require 40% more pages than then; such are the reverses
we all suffer in the 'war on paper'. With more information in the PESC
publications, which link up all forms of public expenditure, and not just

the central government's expenditure on Votes, there would be no point in repeating it in the Estimates and Accounts. The multiplication of detail is often the enemy of effective control. The essence is to get the significant information into the form in which the lay observer can see what is going on.

A radical simplification of Supply procedure would, I think, help towards a change in the traditional doctrine expounded in the textbooks, that the Public Accounts Committee is the watchdog on the department's spending and that the appearance of the Permanent Secretary at the PAC is the occasion on which the department's efficiency is under examination; and that this is a sharp confrontation in which the C & AG's task is to be the critic and the Permanent Secretary's to be the defender. On the contrary, the proper concept to my mind is that the Permanent Secretary should regard the auditor as his ally, to help him find the weak points in the department's systems, and to strengthen them. The operation should be conducted so as to enable him to welcome the discovery of inefficiencies, not to have to stand publicly in the dock to 'explain' them.

If the nature and purpose of the audit were developed in this way, it would call for changes in the institution and the procedures of PAC, C & AG and E & A; and corresponding changes would be needed in the departments. I would envisage the Permanent Secretary being required to submit a regular report on the efficiency of his department's financial procedures and on what was being done to get better value for money; and being examined very searchingly on this report. He would of course be examined in cases discovered by E & A in which he had been personally at fault. In cases which had not come to him personally, it would be desirable to bring in as witnesses the officials who had been responsible, with the crucial final question to the Permanent Secretary on how he proposed to prevent this kind of inefficiency from recurring. For some areas, specified officials would be designated as responsible for this purpose, just as for some Votes now the Accounting Officer is a Second Permanent Secretary or Deputy Secretary.

Such a system would be no less testing for the Permanent Secretary and the department, and would probe the weaknesses more deeply than the present practice; and I would expect it to yield a better return in terms of value for money. It would avoid the tendency for officials down the line to cover up for fear of exposing their Permanent Secretary; and would make it impossible for people in the departments and the Treasury to continue with time-honoured practices for checking or whatever it may be, resisting change by saying that this would be against E & A rules. It would enable (and perhaps push) the Permanent Secretary to do his job better, instead of having to dredge through acres of paper about things that he should never see if he is to manage his business properly.

I have spent time on parliamentary control, because the difficulties of changing it are great and its importance is therefore underrated. Let me be clear that I would not advocate a diminution of parliamentary control. In my opinion, the Executive is too strong in relation to Parliament rather than too weak. But I do believe that changes both for Supply procedure and for audit could be devised which would both strengthen the substance of parliamentary control (while abandoning the shadow) and make a larger impact on the efficiency of the departments' financial administration. It seems incongruous that we should be spending large resources on providing management training and other means of improving the standard of management of the service without exploring these possibilities fully.

Central Management Division

We now come to the central management of the organisation and personnel. In a 'giant' department, this will normally be integrated : indeed, the possibilities of gains from integration are among the arguments for the 'giants', viz to deploy the department's manpower resources better, to widen the career base, to provide better management services, and to get economies of scale in management. In a more 'federal' structure, of course, it would be possible to have the federal units responsible for their own management, with a co-ordinating superstructure, just as each could be responsible for its own finance. In the 'giant' department there are strong arguments for integration here, and for a powerful Central Management Division(s).

A distinction is readily made between the management of personnel and the provision of organisation and management services. In Mintech we had one large Establishment & Management Services Division (EMS), with two Under-Secretaries in joint charge, in order to emphasise that the two halves were engaged in one combined operation, working as one team. The heads of the division worked to the Permanent Secretary (and to the two Second Permanent Secretaries where appropriate) ; and the Establishment and Budget Committee was the centre of the operations. From the start, a great deal of work had to be done in bringing together the differing practices of the constituent departments in each successive merger ; and we had to go through it subject by subject to establish unified practices for the new department.

I would now call this the Central Management Division ; and I think it useful to have new titles in this area just as in finance. In the post-Fulton world, units will be developing which will differ greatly from the old Establishment Division ; and the title should convey this message. Some departments, moreover, have had a bad tradition of rating establishment work too low, and undermanning these divisions, both in numbers and in quality. My predecessors at the old Ministry of Aviation made its Establishment Division a striking exception : its quality when I arrived there in April 1966 is shown by the promotion within the next four years of the Head of the Division to Deputy Secretary and of three of the Assistant Secretaries. The 'giant' department requires strong staffing here ; and in my opinion the required image differs enough from the traditional one to warrant a change of name.

Control of Staff Numbers

This must come first, to keep the total under restraint, and to make it possible to deploy the staff effectively. We are under continuous pressure from the Civil Service Department to reduce our staff, and this must, of course, continue ; and I shall refer to this aspect later. But a 'giant' department will always need to control its numbers, whatever may be the requirements from the centre of government.

The natural course is to give to each division, and thence each branch, a limit within which it must work for a specified period, with an orderly arrangement for dealing with claims for expansion and getting trade-offs by reductions elsewhere, and a long-term plan for examination of requirements so that nobody is able to keep his manpower simply through inertia. A nice judgment is needed in fixing these limits, for the process is self-defeating if the limits are set at levels at which the work cannot be done properly, or if the arrangements for enforcing them are not flexible enough. If their effect is to prevent divisions from increasing their manpower to do things that would save money or manpower, the operation becomes ridiculous. In Mintech we had to be careful to leave enough room to enable the undermanned Contracts Division to recruit all the staff it could, and be flexible enough to let the research establishments take on profitable work for industry ; and however critical the manpower situation, it could not be right to cut back O & M. With a large and diverse staff recruited by units all over the country, we were never able to predict our staff at a given date several months ahead within a margin of less than 1% ; so we could never be absolutely sure of keeping within our estimate except by planning to be substantially below it, and so unnecessarily damaging the department's work. It is only by this continuing pressure, however, applied over the whole department, that total manpower can be kept under control and the economies wrung from the areas of stable and declining work load.[4]

[4] The Mintech outcome was interesting. The department was manned by successive transfers from DSIR (1965), Ministry of Aviation (1967), Board of Trade (1966, 1969), Ministry of Power (1969), Department of Economic Affairs (1969). These acquisitions added up to 25,330 non-industrial staff. The actual number at 1 April 1970 was 25,550 ; and the numbers fell after that date. So the increases and recruitments that we made from the start were offset by rationalisation in the mergers and other economies. Taking into account the reduction in the number of Service staff in the department and in the number of industrial workers, there was an overall saving of about 5% in the period from 1 April 1968 to 1 April 1970.

14

Management Services

The application of management services must be a major force in reducing the department's manpower or in enabling it to do more or better work with the same manpower. I believe that a department needs quite a large capability in order to choose between the range of services now available and get the best value for them. This is fashionable territory with its fair share of charlatans; and one can easily become so sceptical that nothing is ever done, or so enthusiastic that there are altogether too many people analysing how the department is doing its work and criticising it with the only result being one of frustrated exasperation.

The return on well-directed O & M work is certainly favourable. The Civil Service Department's O & M Division, the leader for the whole service, reckons that results can be quantified for about half the assignments undertaken, and that the annual savings achieved have varied between about $2\frac{1}{2}$ and over 10 times the cost of undertaking them. The experience of the Mintech O & M Divisions was much the same.[5] These are returns of between 250 and 1,000% on the resources invested; and even if one debits them with the cost of the non-quantifiable assignments and with the cost of experimental work and the development of new techniques, they are still remarkable returns compared with the yield that can be expected on capital investment in any industry. Such measurement as has been made of the relative efficiency of the civil service and the private sector in doing comparable pieces of work does not suggest that the civil service is the less efficient; and my conclusion which is supported, I think, by the success and expansion of the management consultants is that there are almost always considerable savings to be made from the improvement of organisation and methods, provided that there are skilled and well-trained O & M and related workers to find them, and provided that the customer is willing to co-operate fully. These savings are very large in relation to the resources employed in finding them.

Thus each 'giant' department, in my opinion, should have a long-term plan and the capability to examine every one of its branches—a superficial survey in the first instance, to be followed up by a full-scale review if this seemed likely to yield results—in, say, a five-year period. Our management services are still comparatively small—only $0 \cdot 6\%$ of the service, of whom half are doing computer work: the civil service was a pioneer in introducing O & M in the early 1940s, but now has a smaller management services effort in relation to its size than some of the most progressive firms in the private sector.

It would take time to develop the effort that I suggest above. But I am sure that this is one of the real possibilities for bringing about a reduction

[5] Our assignment teams cost about £80,000 a year: we usually had four or five contracts with consultants on internal jobs, at about £40,000 a year.

in civil service manpower; and I believe it is one of the certain ways of increasing the efficiency and productivity of the Service.

Management of Personnel

We now come to personnel work, which is a combination of the related processes of promotion procedure, career development and training. Its true importance may be expressed in terms of the value of the human capital of the service. When one looks at the civil service as the business of providing governmental services, just as the transport industry is the business of providing transport services or the entertainment industry is the business of providing entertainment services, one very striking feature is its labour intensiveness.

Apart from its buildings, computers, office machinery, research establishments, the assets of the governmental service industry (i.e. the civil service) are its human capital—the accumulated skill and capability of the civil servants. This human capital can be replaced by machines only to a very limited extent. The security of employment is such, moreover, that a decision to employ a man or woman in the late 'teens or early twenties is a 40-year decision; and it is very difficult to correct a mistake. If the quality and the efficiency of the recruitment and development and operation of this human capital can be improved, this is worth great time and effort.

Human Capital

This line of thought was suggested to me by the chairman of a very successful company in an advanced technological industry. A statement that showed the real worth and earning potential of a company, he said, would be bound to include the human assets as well as the physical. The physical assets are the factories and research establishments; but the real future depends upon the quality of the men who judge what the public will want, who can discern the next technological stage, and who can assess how the company should develop and deploy its effort world-wide. Everyone in top management knows that this is so, and great efforts are made to find the best men and to make the best use of them; and it is unquestionably possible to attribute a value to each of these men. Of course, a balance sheet comprising both the human and the physical assets would be a different kind of statement from the conventional one (the company does not own the human assets!); but it could be more important than the conventional one for assessing the company's real capability.

An analogous strand of thought was developed in his youth by the Australian industrialist and founder of the metal industry there, Mr W S Robinson. I quote from his memoirs:[6]

[6] *'If I Remember Rightly', The Memoirs of W S Robinson 1876–1963*. Edited by Geoffrey Blainey. Published by F W Cheshire, Melbourne, Canberra, Sydney.

'When I entered industry in 1914 I was struck by the care devoted to inanimate power and the carelessness displayed to manpower. The machine was carefully selected on expert advice, submitted to severe tests, and splendidly housed. It had an army of attendants to feed it, to keep it in constant repair and to polish it. Manpower, however, was not infrequently "taken on at the gate" from the crowds milling round looking for jobs. No attention was paid to housing, or to transport to and from work, or to feeding or hospitalisation, or educational facilities for a man's children or amenities for his wife . . . As soon as possible I introduced the slogan, "*At least* as much care for the man as for the machine, . . ." '

He goes on to describe the battle to improve the conditions both in Australia and in New South Wales ; but the relevant point to my argument is his analogy between the handling of physical assets and human assets.

The figures quoted above of the return of 250 to 1,000% on resources devoted to O & M work illustrate again the immense scope for applying resources to improve the human capital, compared with the return on the improvement of the physical assets.

One might perhaps measure this 'human capital' as the present value of the future earnings of present civil servants. Including both non-industrials and industrials (although the considerations above apply somewhat less strongly to the latter), I would put this at something of the order of £10,000 million. For comparison, the aggregate of the net physical assets of the nationalised industries is of the order of £15,000 million. We should think very seriously and continuously about how to make the best possible use of the human assets that constitute the civil service. I put this in deliberately sharp and 'economic' terms, because there is much more in this than the duty, important though this be, for the government to be a good employer. This is a different dimension of argument.

There is, as I see it, a clear common interest here between the management of the service and the 700,000 non-industrial and industrial civil servants. In the 'giant' department, there is both a great opportunity to develop effective and constructive personnel management policies, and a positive need to do so.

Promotion Procedure

This is a well-established structure, firmly embedded in the Whitley Council system. In the 'giant' department, the procedure must be more formalised than in a smaller one. An important question is that of the handling of the posts in the top area of unification of the service, at Under-Secretary level and above, and of the posts at the next level below (Assistant Secretary and equivalent). At each level at which unification takes place, the system of separate promotion machinery within each class—'scientists managed by scientists'—will disappear and be replaced by machinery which handles all classes or occupational groups at that level together. These new procedures must carry the full support and confidence of everybody in the department; which is why If avour formally involving the whole top echelon in them.

In Mintech we were operating 'opportunity posting' from 1965 onward; and we were continually bringing in staff from other departments and other backgrounds; and our experience may be of value. Postings at Under-Secretary (or equivalent) level, and promotions to that level, are clearly the responsibility of the Permanent Secretary;[7] and they are so crucial to the department that it was always my practice to submit them to the Minister. We sometimes decided first in the Establishment and Budget Committee whether we wanted a scientist or an administrator for a particular post: we sometimes set up a panel with instructions about the sort of man to look for and sometimes with a completely free hand. Often we had to deal with several posts simultaneously. With about 80 posts at this level,[8] fairly equally divided between administrators and scientists, there was a continuous flow of vacancies to be filled; but the operation was readily manageable.

Postings at Assistant Secretary and equivalent level—in 'last Mintech', there were 290 of them—and promotions to that level, cannot be initiated by the Permanent Secretary, although he will require to approve them, and in a great many cases will know a lot about them. This is where the difference in scale is important. In my opinion, a formal promotion board procedure is needed at this level for each occupational group (as has been the case for scientists and engineers in the departments which employ a lot); and the top management will need to define which posts should be filled from particular occupational groups and which should be regarded as open to all, with a mixed promotion board. This can be a difficult level to handle in the 'giant' department with a unified class structure.

Career Development

The purpose of career development machinery is to build up the long-term capability of the staff. In the higher grades, where it can deal with individuals, it provides the background of systematic knowledge of the staff and their individual capabilities to guide the promotion panels, and to get a sense of what one might call strategic direction into the process. But it should be kept separate from the day-to-day promotion decisions; for the latter are concerned with particular situations.

There are advantages in scale here. The Defence Services do career

[7] Appointments at the Deputy Secretary level are handled by machinery covering the whole Service, and require the Prime Minister's approval.
[8] Including CSO(B)'s.

development well ; and the large numbers of scientists employed by the old Ministries of Supply and Aviation were better handled than in most of the civil service. The danger point for size comes when the career development organisation itself becomes so large that it cannot fit easily into the personnel organisation generally, and becomes a separate specialist subject.

Working down from the top of a department, the Under-Secretary (and equivalent) will always be under close surveillance by top management, and his career development within a department presents no special problems. He will become part of the unified all-service 'senior policy and management group', and his prospects will be considered accordingly.

The Assistant Secretary level is normally about the highest for which formal departmental career development procedure is necessary. The 290 in 'last Mintech' were divided about equally between generalists and specialists. We decided upon a two-yearly 'Promotion Potential Review' conducted by the Permanent Secretary with a varying core of the Establishment and Budget Committee (who could all attend if they wished). We had four categories :

A Promotable within two years
B Promotable in two to five years
C Promotable after five years
D Unlikely to be promoted

Each man's immediate superior put in a note giving his opinion of the man's category. We then had meetings, considering about 20 at each meeting, with the relevant heads of divisions (Under-Secretaries etc) present, grouping the cases so that we had an adequate number there who would know each man. At the end of the discussion the Permanent Secretary would write a short note for the record on each man, giving the agreed category, and any particular points about re-posting or further consideration that were required.

We thus had a ready-made field in category A whenever a vacancy for promotion arose (though we sometimes included in the field special 'horses for courses'). We could see well in advance whether we needed to take action on people in B and C. In considering the scientists and engineers, we took particular care to pick out those who could take on wider 'general' responsibilities. Perhaps the most significant field was D. The Assistant Secretary grade is the career level for most of the Administrative Class, with duties carrying high responsibility and pay rising to £6,300 (June 1971). By definition, the majority will never get higher. It is useful to identify them—though this does not affect their prospects if they do better. What we must look out for is the possibility that an Assistant Secretary aged 50, with no likelihood of promotion, may slip back in his performance and even become a serious problem ; and that good posting could prevent this. In terms of our 'human capital' this category is large, for the last ten years of an Assistant Secretary's working life make up nearly one-third of his career earnings ; and if he can be put into the right niche, this is of major importance. I hope we may turn out to have taken useful action here.

In autumn 1970, we were just completing the first cycle, having incorporated the newcomers from the merger of October 1969. With 290, the cycle must be two-yearly, but this is enough. I believe that this kind of systematic process is more likely to be effective than more informal processes in smaller departments.

General Service Classes

At the next level, the numbers become large, and 'career development' begins to require definition. It must be handled separately in occupational groups—administrative/executive/clerical, scientist/engineer, accountant etc. Below a certain level (which we put at Senior Executive Officer on the 'general service' side) the numbers become too large to handle individually in a central organisation. In the scientific and engineer classes, people below Principal Scientific Officer must be handled in the research establishments and in HQ divisions ; and there must be a decentralised system in the technical class.

The projected system in Mintech for the 'general classes', which broke entirely new ground, and had been announced to take effect on 1 October 1970, sought to create a practical plan for very large numbers. A steering group was to be set up under a Deputy Secretary, with nine panels. The first would be for the top group, about 300 SCEOs, Principals and CEOs—and would also advise the Permanent Secretary on promotions from that level. The second was for Senior Executive Officers, about 300. There were four panels to handle about 3,000 HEOs and EOs : these were divided by age group, i.e. 50 and over, 41–49, 28–40, and under 28. We thought that the root of the career development problem was the problems of executives in the relatively junior grades at different ages ; and we therefore organised in age groups. Similarly there would be three panels (ages 50 and over, 30–49 and under 30) for the nearly 5,000 people in the clerical classes.

The panels dealing with the older executive age groups dealt with about 1,000 each ; the two younger groups with 550 each. This gave the panels dealing with people in the formative stages of their careers more scope for individual attention. As the patterns of careers become settled people change their jobs less often, and need proportionately less individual attention. This was experimental, and the age boundaries will no doubt need to be considered in the light of experience ; age 32 may become the boundary (instead of 28) as it is now the upper limit

20

of consideration of internal candidates for selection for the grade of Administration Trainee.

This system is still in its early stages. At the top end, it is possible to consider career development in terms of the handling of individuals: at the bottom in the large panels it is necessary to think systematically in terms of the problems of the career development of large numbers of people. I think we may well find that the latter process will contribute at least as much to the growth in the human capital of the service. I believe that our present system performs well in picking out people for promotion and moving them up the ladders: I am more impressed with the need to make the very most of the capabilities of the great majority.

In my opinion, in times of stress, many people are capable of performing well above the level of their grade. This was obviously true in World War II. But I have always noticed, too, how well people do when their seniors are away sick or on leave; and I believe that we tend to employ people a little below their capabilities. The problem is to make more effective use of those who are not likely to be promoted; and this is worth much thought and attention.

Administrative Specialisation

An alternative way of looking at the problems of the general service classes below the Assistant Secretary level is to handle them in terms of administrative specialisation, dividing the work of the department up into chunks and having one career apparatus for contracts and related work, one for financial administration, one for management services etc. This would lead to greater professional expertise. But it carries with it great risk of increasing rigidity and inflexibility: the trend is towards multidisciplinary activity, and a wide ranging transferability of staff is good for that. Moreover, if there is to be specialisation, the size of each specialist area must be large enough to give a sufficient career potential base for those in it; it is only rarely in the civil service that one can find such a base. In 'last Mintech' after tremendous analysis, it proved impossible to do so; and so the idea of dividing the general service class into a number of categories for career specialisation was abandoned.

The problem of inadequate expertise is, of course, still there. But the answer may be found not in seeking to define a man's specialisation for his whole working life early in his career, but in making the normal postings for a longer period of years. If a man takes six months to learn a job, and a year to become really effective in it, then if he has one job instead of two in four years his 'output' over that period will be raised by about 25%. If management seeks to put a brake on the number of changes of job; and regards specialisation as reasonable without making a shibboleth of it, this may ultimately give the best results.

Scientists and Engineers

For the scientists and engineers, specialisation is much sharper ; and the career development system, which has in essence been in existence for many years, is a series of five panels, each headed by a Deputy Controller, for each of the main technical areas, covering the SPSOs and PSOs, and specifically providing that the position of staff below that level is reviewed in the research establishments. The new element here is an attempt to distinguish young men in the research establishments, by whether their best prospects are likely to be in HQ technical or industrial administration, in local management, or in continuing research work.

The success of this identification will in the long run determine the possibility of bringing more scientists into administrative work. If they are going to get on to the ladders to the top administrative posts, they will need to get their training and start getting their administrative experience certainly by their middle 30s. There is quite a close analogy to the transfer of able scientists and engineers in industry on to the business management side sufficiently early in their career. In Mintech, we looked searchingly for this ability among the scientists and engineers who had reached the 'Promotion Potential Review', and some have reached administrative positions of Under-Secretary rank or higher. But to use the potential resources effectively, they need to be picked out much earlier.

Administration Trainees

When the expanded graduate intake begins, it will be impossible to give as much individual attention to the new grade of Administration Trainee, as top management previously gave to the handful of Assistant Principals. But our experience with the larger numbers in the 'giant' department may help. In old Aviation, and then in Mintech, an Under-Secretary acted as 'guide, philosopher and friend' to the Assistant Principals—a man outside the establishment division and hierarchy, to keep an eye on their progress and welfare, and a useful consultant for the Permanent Secretary when their collective problems were in mind. One such guide for every 10–15 Administration Trainees can make a big contribution. Another device was a substantial annual meeting of the Assistant Principals (34 in 'last Mintech') with the Permanent Secretaries to discuss an agenda dealing with the objectives and management problems of the department.

The greater width of the 'giant' department, however, has advantages for the training of the new entrants. Where the department has a regional organisation, this gives a valuable opportunity to give the new entrant at least a year's experience at the grass roots of the department's work, whether this be industrial, environmental or social service. This is particularly valuable for those brought up in the South, trained at Oxbridge or 'Plateglass', and often ignorant of the industrial areas. My own hope is that no one will be able to reach a high position in an industrial department without experience of working in an industrial area.

Training

The provision of training must be closely allied to career development, both in the handling of individuals and in examining the needs of particular grades at different ages. For example, the idea of enabling the specialist, aged around 35, to move into more general administration as well as into management work within his own professional discipline depends entirely upon the provision of the right kind of training arrangements. Bearing in mind the immense changes which take place in every civil servant's lifetime, moreover, there is a major problem of renovating each civil servant's equipment, decade by decade, and this, too, is a function of training.

In my opinion it is possible greatly to improve the work and to speed the learning process by directed training in departments. I am concerned here with training provided within the department, and not with the central courses provided by the Civil Service College, or with courses at the Administrative Staff College at Henley or the business schools or other outside establishments; though the selection of people for these courses is an important part of the department's training and career development work. There is room for discussion about balance between the department's courses, which will necessarily form the bulk of the total provision, and which will normally be tailored to the department's specific needs; the courses provided by the Civil Service College, which will be related to the needs of the service but which will be designed to introduce broader concepts; and the outside courses, which are not directed to civil service needs at all, and much of the value of which consists of the contact with industry and with other professions.

Some departments do their training work very well. The quality of the Inland Revenue's work is proverbial. The training in the old Aviation Contracts Division is very good. But where the work is less clearly defined, it is more difficult to formulate the training schemes, though no less important (indeed, perhaps more so). To work in an industry division effectively, everyone needs to know how to look at a balance sheet, the sources of industrial finance, the elements of industrial structure; and in other big blocks of departmental work there is just the same kind of basic need. It is constructive to be able to put new entrants into these divisions through short courses of this character. It is even better if these are reinforced by the existence of documents which set out the recent history and background of major matters in the division's work—the 'funding of experience'. There is a problem in getting such documents prepared—the Treasury put a significant effort into this in the late 1950s and something was done in the old Aviation Department and in Mintech, and no doubt in other departments. But the combination of a course on the elements of the work of each type of division and documents on the background of the division's work can speed up by months the time that a man takes to become an effective member of a division.

This can be done only when the training programmes are closely related to the needs of the operating divisions. The training organisation can easily become something of an enclave in the department, proceeding with the training as an objective in itself, and separated from the department's actual needs. In 'second Mintech', our Training Division, another inheritance from Aviation, had a staff of over 50 people, engaged in a training effort which absorbed 2·3% of the non-industrial staff's aggregate working time—at least 50% above the Whitehall average. This was largely for the scientific and technical grades, and there were great differences in the amount of training provided in different parts of the department, and a good deal of criticism. We set up a major review by a strong Training Review Group selected to represent the needs of the whole department and chaired by a Deputy Secretary. This was a tremendous job; but it resulted in a reshaping of the organisation and direction of the effort, with an Assistant Secretary put in charge, and the appointment of a Steering Committee under a Deputy Secretary and a continuing organisation of panels, the whole designed to keep the training work continuously related to the operating divisions' needs. The 'giant' department is in a very strong position to provide departmental training over a wide range of subjects; but it is essential that the control of the training effort in terms of substance should be kept on the operational side of the department and should not be simply a 'management' function, as if 'training' was a purpose in itself.

Personnel and Line Management

Throughout personnel work, the essential is to build upon the work and interest of the operating divisions (or line-management). The promotion panels, the career development panels, the training panels must all be manned by the people who are responsible for the day-to-day work of the department. The Central Management Division provides the central apparatus for arranging and presenting the work of these panels; and the way in which the 'line' and 'staff' roles are combined is decisive.

Quite a significant proportion of the Under-Secretaries (and equivalents) should therefore be directly involved in the personnel management of the department, whether in promotion, career development or training activities. This is indispensable for the success of the personnel functions, which cannot be carried out exclusively by people who are not involved in the day-to-day operations of the department: it is also a powerful force for the integration of the department, as it leads the senior people in the department to think not only about their own particular segment (which civil servants very properly tend to do) but about the needs of the department as a whole.

Communication and Integration

Another fashionable word, describing a real problem in the 'giant' department. First, does the 'giant' department drive decisions upward in the organisation? If there are 15 people at Deputy Secretary level, some people say the Minister will look to them, and the Under-Secretaries will be squeezed out. If so, there is a real danger. The Under-Secretaries are the kingpins of the modern department. They are the people with knowledge of and contact with industry or local government or whatever the subject matter may be; and if they are superseded in the Minister's decision-making, this destroys the expert contribution of the department. The normal practice should therefore be for the Under-Secretaries to make their submissions direct to Ministers, and for the Deputy Secretaries and Permanent Secretaries to intervene only when it is absolutely necessary or, of course, when the Under-Secretary wants them to intervene. This was all set out agreeably and clearly in a circular to the Foreign and Commonwealth Office by Sir Paul Gore-Booth in the early days of that 'giant' department (Annex 3).

Secondly, does the formal organisation on paper in the charts and functional directories in fact correspond to the organisation in practice? In a small department, this does not matter very much, for the actual practice is clear to everyone (or should be). But in a 'giant' department it is difficult for anyone to keep the structure in mind; and therefore the charts and the functional directories and the like are of first-class practical importance; for people actually use them. The written word and the written instruction become more important. This is why I attach weight to getting new titles which correspond to new functions.

Thirdly, who knows whether the way in which the work is done and the relations between the staffs who are doing it is in fact the same as the higher management believes it to be? The top people in any but the smallest organisation will probably be ignorant of the way in which the organisation actually works. They may be under a complete misunderstanding of the actual flow of talk and paper down the line. One of the most important tasks of the higher management, in my opinion, is to devise means of obtaining this understanding. In Mintech this question was far from solved. I am not convinced that anyone in Whitehall (and very few anywhere else) has yet solved it. But I know that attempts are under way.

3

Fourthly, how do we bring about the psychological integration of the 'giant' department? The pace of change in the civil service has been such that traditional patterns of thought are less firmly rooted than they were recently. Without stability in machinery of government, it is counter-productive to try to build up a strong loyalty to a department. Nevertheless, the integration must take place in the minds of at any rate the senior staff before it can be embodied in the work. The question of accommodation is of first-class importance. 'Last Mintech' was in 26 buildings in Central London, and this was a tremendous obstacle, both practically in getting an effective communication system within the department and psychologically: this was perhaps the most serious difficulty of all.

This must be a particular task for the Permanent Secretary. I asked for copies of all the submissions to Ministers, and would react quite sharply whenever anyone wrote a submission which was parochial in tone and failed to appreciate the full width of the department's interests. I held regular meetings with the Under-Secretaries in mixed batches, not to discuss current business, but to consider general long-range policy. Every year I gave addresses to about eight groups each of several score of staff, in order to explain and answer questions about what we were trying to do. The direct work with the Whitley Council staff side can contribute a lot, especially as the mergers of departments face them with difficult merger problems too. We tried to make the office circulars more informative, and conducted campaigns like 'war on paper'. We were embarking upon a series of social gatherings designed to mix up the senior staff and to help to get them to know each other. The house-journal has a big role to play, the sports side too, and so on.

My opinion in retrospect is that we did not do enough. The then Minister, Mr Wedgwood Benn, made some very valuable contributions; and judged by normal civil service practice we all devoted a large effort to this task of unification. But I believe that it may be found desirable to allocate some specific responsibility for this. It is part of the personnel work of the department, but it is not part of the normal personnel management function; and I think there is an unsolved problem here. In a 'giant' department, I do not think we can rely on waking up in two years' time and saying 'Hurrah, boys, we've integrated'. The communication and integration problems continue.

Administrators and Scientists

The original Mintech was organised in 1965 with a single structure, and administrators, scientists and engineers working in the same organisational pyramid, and all the posts were in principle 'opportunity posts'. The Ministry of Aviation, on the other hand, was organised in the traditional double pyramid of hierarchies; an organisation of engineers and scientists leading up to the Controller (Aircraft) and the Controller

(Guided Weapons and Electronics) at Deputy Secretary level, and an organisation of administrators leading up to Deputy Secretaries. Historically this system was designed to ensure that at each stage there was a financial check upon the work of the engineers and scientists, who were, as the slogan went 'on tap but not on top'.

In the last 15 years, this situation has in practice been radically changed. It became accepted that the system, by taking financial decisions out of the engineers' hands, increased the danger of financial irresponsibility. So in the control of each aviation project (usually led by an engineer) the financial control was included with all the other elements of control. At the peak of the pyramid, CA and CGWL became responsible for the financial aspects of projects, and the financial branches (manned by administrators) became in practice part of the organisation responsible to CA and CGWL, with the Deputy Secretaries acting alongside, dividing up with them the practical work to be done at that level, almost all an inextricable mixture of technical, industrial and financial work.

In theory there were two hierarchies, one administrative and one technical. In practice it became a single organisation with a differentiation of functions between the men of different skills with the top posts filled on 'opportunity' lines. The most recent appointments (November 1970) in the Ministry of Aviation Supply filled the Deputy Secretary post for civil aircraft with an engineer, and the Head of the Concorde Division with an administrator.

The experience has shown that it is possible by a variety of routes to get working structures with administrators, scientists and engineers all in one team, and with the top posts open to the best man irrespective of background, in fact as well as in principle. One cannot say how far this will extend ; but it may not be unreasonable to hope that a problem which was very sensitive ten years ago, is on the way to solution.[9]

Research Establishments

Under the arrangements proposed in Cmnd 4506, most of the government's research and development will be in the organisation dealing with defence procurement and aerospace. But both the Department of the Environment and the Department of Trade and Industry have large scientific research activities, and their own establishments (and, in the case of DTI, the AEA establishments) ; and this is a problem of management in itself. I am not here concerned whether this work is best done in government establishments, in industry or elsewhere. I assume that government research establishments exist, and the question is how to manage them.

An awkward balance must be struck between giving the research establishment such a free hand that it interests itself in academic

[9] The structure of the Procurement Organisation in the Ministry of Defence is another great step forward.

problems and is useless to the department's work and the exact opposite, which is to dominate the research establishment's work from the centre to such a degree that it really ceases to be a scientific research establishment at all. This problem presents itself differently depending on the work of the department. The defence/aerospace research establishments are an integral part of the government's defence/aerospace procurement process; but the industrial and environmental ones have only limited direct involvement in the department's work. So the department's control over the research establishments' programmes will differ considerably.

In my opinion a department with a substantial scientific research involvement (with research establishments of its own) will always need a Chief Scientist or Controller (Research) or whatever title may be appropriate, who will be in charge of the whole research effort of the department and the allocation of resources between intra-mural and extra-mural work and, within the intra-mural sector, between the various establishments. He is needed for this administrative function; but he is also needed to handle the department's scientific affairs in the wider national and international setting; and to be the professional head of the department's own scientists, to give professional leadership and to guide the promotion, career development and training work of the department's scientists. Both his functions in relation to the outside world and that of leading and managing the department's scientists are of great importance, and largely determine the department's standing with the national and international scientific community.

Under the Controller (Research) there must be a suitable organisation to coordinate and guide the programmes of the research establishments (closely in some cases and much less so in others, but in all cases leaving a certain element of the programme to be set up by the establishment director himself); and to manage the central control of their personnel and finance, in close association with the Central Management and Budget Divisions. At one time it was thought that this should all be done by scientists, but this concept is out of date.

One purpose of the 'second Mintech' merger of February 1967 was to bring together the strategy of developing and deploying the large R & D effort of these departments (17 research establishments plus AEA, which was as big as all the rest put together). A Research Group was set up accordingly, under a Controller (Research). It was clear from the start that the intensity of HQ control of the establishments' work and programmes would differ widely according to their establishments' involvement in the department's day-to-day activity.

But it was not necessary that this should apply to their responsibility for their own personnel and finance; and we therefore embarked upon a major review of how the relationship between HQ and the research establishments should be developed. We began with the intention of putting the maximum possible responsibility upon the directors of research establishments; and of putting the onus on HQ to prove the justification of every control exercised by HQ over the establishment.

This operation began in spring 1968, and took two years to carry out; for it was necessary to consult closely with the directors of research establishments (who were not unanimously in favour of greater freedom and greater responsibility) and to examine the practice of comparable organisations in the private and public sectors and overseas. The changes of autumn 1970 broke up the structure of the Mintech research establishments (between Ministry of Aviation Supply, Department of Trade and Industry, and Department of the Environment) before this process was completed, but important changes had been made, which are likely to survive with the new situation:

(i)   The articulation of the procedure for determination of the establishment's programme by HQ with the procedure for determining manpower and budget and capital expenditure limits.

(ii)   Maximum autonomy for the research establishment in personnel matters, to the extent consistent with the fact that the department is the employer of all personnel, and that therefore there must be reasonable consistency of practice throughout the research establishments (and with HQ) and at the higher levels participation in the department's arrangements for promotion, career development and training. It is difficult to strike a balance, but we were able to increase the establishments' freedom of action significantly.

(iii)   Likewise for finance, the main problem here being in the smaller establishments.

(iv)   The removal of a great many controls, the outcome of several years' rules in the history of the constituent departments (Air Ministry, War Office, DSIR etc), mostly reasonable in themselves, but in the aggregate giving rise to much irritation and weakening of the establishment's own sense of responsibility.[10]

These arrangements, if sustained by the successor departments and extended to other establishments within their control, would represent a valuable step forward towards a greater responsibility for directors of research establishments. I had envisaged that in future years the director of the research establishment would accompany the Permanent Secretary to the Public Accounts Committee if any question arose about his stewardship. This increase in responsibility and accountability must match the increased freedom of action; and both are under considerable restraint for as long as the research establishments are part of departments, both as regards staff and money.

[10] e.g. powers (and responsibility) for write-offs, authority to make contracts, purchase of periodicals, approval of overseas travel, use of their own vehicles, ordering stationery, employment of lecturers, approval of payment to staff for time lost, fees for authors, authorisation of open days etc.

Regional Organisation

The 'giant' department is likely to have a regional organisation, which in my opinion is likely to become increasingly important to its work. In the industrial, environmental or social service fields the creation of the 'giant' department and the merging of its operations in the regions can change the nature of the work in the regions. In a relatively small department, the regional organisation will be a simple one, aimed simply at carrying out HQ instructions on a particular subject. But with the 'giant' department combining together many regional tasks of its constituent departments, the regional organisation becomes a microcosm of the department as a whole, and the representative of the department in the region.

Moreover, the regional organisation may be able to take on functions from the centre : in 'last Mintech' I envisaged that they would ultimately have a bigger role in relation to the government's policy towards small and medium-sized firms. When the departments become large and comprehensive in their responsibilities in respect of wide segments of the national life, it becomes necessary, in my opinion, to avoid the proliferation at the centre and to do as much as possible in the regions if government contacts are to be real and government action effective.

These considerations are independent of whether there is a move towards 'regional government' or 'regional planning'. It follows from the widening of the field of activity of the 'giant' department, the danger of bureaucratic inertia if an attempt is made to run everything from Whitehall, and the need for the 'giant' department to have a contact and life of its own throughout the country. This also helps not only to create a nation-wide presence for the department, but also to bring about its integration into an effective instrument of government.

The Department's Public

I must continue from regional organisations and the nation-wide presence of the department to its contact with public opinion. I am concerned here with the two-way contact between the department and its own public—the organisations and interests and institutions within the department's field of responsibility. This is much affected by the department's general public-relations image as shown by the press and television ; but all I need say about this is that there is no substitute for the speeches of Ministers and the normal day-to-day professional apparatus of public relations and publicity work. Mr Wedgwood Benn ranked this high, and developed some original techniques for creating a better understanding in selected newspapers and other communication media of what the department was trying to do ; and this had, I thought, some degree of success. But there is a simple limit on what can be done along these lines, dictated by the individual capability of the department's ministers, and the amount of time and effort that they can devote to this kind of work.

For the 'giant' department, its 'own public' is formidably large. *Whitaker's Almanack* lists over 1,500 societies, institutions, associations, and professional organisations covering the whole of the national life; and DTI and DOE must know a great many of them. These are among the crucial opinion-forming areas; and each department's contact with the various bodies within its own fields of business must be one of its most important tasks. It is here also that government can best refute the charge of 'remoteness'; and I think there is advantage to be derived from encouraging officials at all levels to forge the closest personal links they can with the multitude of organisations within their scope. There is a potential conflict between this view and the more traditional view that if officials' contacts with such organisations are too close this may prejudice the officials' objectivity and independence if the organisations become involved in negotiation with the department. There is a balance to be struck here, but my own belief is that when government reaches its present size and ubiquity, the need for the officials and the neighbouring organisations to know each other and understand each others' point of view is the overriding one.

A related question is that of advisory committees. In every department there are many operations which cannot be carried out sensibly without an outside advisory committee of industrialists, representatives of professional institutions, etc. I am not concerned with these. But there are also advisory committees for which the need is much less definite, but which have a function of maintaining a contact between the Minister or the department and opinion outside. In Mintech, for example, we had an Advisory Council on Technology consisting of industrialists, scientists, university people etc, which had regular meetings with the Ministers and top officials, never to negotiate or to decide anything, but to discuss. In fact, some important policies grew out of these discussions; but the meetings took a lot of time, and it was always possible to argue that their benefit did not outweigh their opportunity cost. In the whole of government there are many such organisations.

If the weakness of 'big government' is that it tends to be too self-centred and remote from the outside world, then it may be wise to create such opportunities for regular contact outside the normal day-to-day business. If on the other hand the real problem is the pressure on time at the top and the need to narrow the department's commitments, then the argument may run the other way. I personally rank high the danger of remoteness in government and absence of feedback; and I am always impressed by the lack of knowledge and understanding of government work by all outside Whitehall except a very few individuals who maintain close contacts with government. My own prejudice would tend to favour the former course, but this is in practice a matter of degree.

It does seem to me, however, that experience since the end of the war shows that government has great difficulty in getting public support and understanding for its policies without the assistance of powerful and vociferous outside bodies—the education boom from the mid-1950s was a most striking case; and it may not be unduly fanciful to say that the existence of a powerful anti-inflation organisation or lobby, outside the government and independent of it, could be a major new force in that situation. It seems to me that the ability of the 'giant' departments to find support outside for their policies will be a very important factor in their success.

The Prospects of 'Giant' Departments

In my opinion, the main problem of the 'giant' department is to get the right amount of centralisation or integration. If there is no integration, there is no sense in setting up a 'giant' department at all. If artificial attempts are made to create integration, and decisions are centralised where this is not clearly necessary for managment, the organisation will be at great risk of seizing up. In my judgment, the right course is to integrate some areas effectively—notably personnel and management services and allocation of financial and other resources, and decisions on the objectives and priorities of the department. This area may widen, but decision-making should nevertheless be kept nearer the periphery, for over-centralisation of policy decisions will in the end be self-defeating. I would rather centralise too little than too much.

I must emphasise once more that the benefits depend upon the stability of the department. The issues of policy and priorities and personnel management must be tailored to the area of the department's responsibility. If this area is changed, then the priorities which were ruling cease to have any meaning, and the whole capacity of the organisation to increase and improve the value of the human capital which is the 'giant' department's great asset likewise ceases to be relevant. In my view, the weight of argument strongly favours having a few 'giant' departments as against a lot of small ones. But these advantages will vanish, and indeed turn into very large disadvantages, unless the stability of the size and structure of the 'giant' departments can be maintained.

As the 'giant' departments become established, the question will arise whether they should be bigger still. Let me illustrate the point with some hypothetical cases (with which I would not agree). Should the Department of Employment be merged into the Department of Trade and Industry? Is it not anomalous to have two Cabinet Ministers and two departments, one responsible for the government's relations with industry and the other responsible for the government's relations with the biggest of all the industrial problems—the relations between management and labour? Or again, should the Ministry of Agriculture, Fisheries and Food be merged with the Department of Trade and Industry? The agricultural industry represents only about $3\frac{1}{2}$% of the nation's labour force and gross national product, which does not in itself justify separate treatment. The food and drink industries are manufacturing industries just like all others (with much bigger employment and income than agriculture); and the role of food products in our international trade is of great importance; and it might well be thought that these were naturally brigaded with the Department of Trade and Industry.

I am making no such proposals, but I must record that President Nixon's new machinery of government proposals would bring into one Department of Economic Development not only the Departments of Commerce and Labor but also the farm programme of the Department of Agriculture (and some else besides)—in pursuit of a policy of organising around 'the great purposes of government' instead of having particular departments for particular narrow subjects and interests.[11]

However this may be, the arguments for further mergers are very much the same as those which justified the setting-up of the Department of Trade and Industry and the Department of the Environment—such mergers would permit a wider view to be taken of the priorities and strategy in each field, and would avoid the need for cumbersome interdepartmental argument. Indeed, such mergers, by widening the subject matter of the government's day-to-day relations with the trade unions in the first example, and by weakening the representation of the agricultural interest in the Cabinet on the other, could lead almost unobtrusively to major changes of national policy.

The argument turns on where the limits are, and especially on two factors, one 'politics' and the other 'management'. For 'politics' the limit is the extent of the subjects that the Minister must handle in the Cabinet and in Parliament, their political sensitivity, and the Minister's capability to handle them well. Over a long period, moreover, it is not a particularly talented Minister that must be considered, but a man or woman of the normal quality of the top ten or dozen in any administration. The Minister must work also with a team of colleagues in the department, two of whom will probably be within the top 20–25 in the administration, and political forces, present or future, in their own right; the Minister's task of working with them and devolving responsibility upon them will depend heavily upon the political sensitivity of the subject matter. So I would put width (not depth) and political sensitivity of the department's work as being the main 'political' consideration; and I would regard this as overriding.

For 'management', I would not regard the sheer numbers of staff and

[11] President Nixon would reduce the number of departments to eight—State, Treasury, Justice, Defence and four new consolidations viz. Natural Resources, Human Resources, Economic Development, Community Development. *Economist.* 30 January 1971, page 39.

public expenditure as being very important. The Inland Revenue and the Department of Health and Social Security both have staffs of about 70,000 ; but are clearly not too big. The diversity of staff and expenditure are more important. A better guide than the number of staff is the number of Under-Secretaries and people of equivalent rank at HQ, which tends to express both the width of the department and the occupational diversity. Or perhaps even the number of Deputy Secretaries and equivalent rank may be the best measure. The number of Permanent Secretaries and Deputy Secretaries and equivalent may be the simplest guide ; and there would be good sense in taking the numbers of parliamentary questions answered by Ministers of various departments year by year in order to get some rough indication of the political sensitivity of their subject ; this could be analysed between the different parts of each department's work (to see what might happen if the department were split up). In the cases shown above, in January 1971, DTI had 20 Permanent and Deputy Secretaries and equivalent, and DOE 19. 'Last Mintech' had 17 (including two heads of research establishments). In relation to the fantasy mergers discussed earlier, note that the Department of Employment has 5 and MAFF has 6.

If the government could remove certain subjects from political considera- tion either by 'hiving-off' or by cutting out functions altogether or by deciding never to intervene in certain areas, the width of the Minister's charge would be reduced and it would become possible to take more subjects into one department. But this would take considerable time and political activity within the Cabinet and in Parliament if it were hoped to move subjects out of the political arena where these are at all sensitive and involve a significant load on the Minister. Over a period of years there could be some relief by this route, but it would probably increase the short- and medium-term load.

When the 'giant' departments have settled down, these limits upon size may tend to widen. But my own experience has been that it takes two years to weld a department of considerable size together, and it probably takes five years to make it a real established entity ; so all this takes a lot of time, and requires a lot of stability to give it a fair chance.

When I was asked in September 1969 whether it would be practicable to merge the 'second Mintech' with the Ministry of Power and large chunks of the Board of Trade and DEA, I had no doubt whatever in saying that it was practicable, and although it was a surprising concept I quickly came to the opinion, on consideration, that it could have great merits and advantages ; and I have never had reason to doubt this view in the light of experience. The scale was three Permanent Secretaries and twelve Deputy Secretaries and equivalent at HQ (and two at research establishments) and a low political sensitivity in the work in relation to the Department's size.

34

When the new ideas developed in the summer of 1970 to merge the 'last Mintech' with the Board of Trade, I was in no doubt whatever that the practical limit had been reached, and that if this new merger were to take place, a large part of the existing functions and organisation would have to go elsewhere. This has, of course, happened ; and until we have more experience of the working of the new 'giant' departments I shall be inclined to stand by this view that something like the limit has been reached, at any rate for the next few years.

II The Centre of Government

We are in sight of having nine (or perhaps ten) major departments in
Whitehall, apart from the Treasury (and the revenue departments) and
the Civil Service Department in the centre :

Foreign and Commonwealth Office (including Overseas Develop-
ment) (FCO)
Defence (MOD)
Trade and Industry (DTI)
Environment (DOE)
Health and Social Security (DHSS)
Education and Science (DES)
Home Office
Employment (DE)
Agriculture, Fisheries and Food (MAFF)

The tenth is the Scottish Office, in an ambiguous position in this analysis,
for its programmes, priorities and allocations are closely related to those
of the English departments ; and its activity is thus different in kind from
the others. It was assumed in the lecture that the Ministry of Aviation
Supply would in spring 1972 cease to be an independent department of
its own, and would be absorbed into a new defence procurement organisation (for these purposes under the Secretary of State for Defence)
with the civil aircraft functions transfered to DTI and this did actually
happen in spring 1971. The Ministry of Posts and Telecommunications,
a department with narrow width though large responsibilities in depth,
may also ultimately be absorbed by one of the major nine departments.

These are changes of great scale which create a new kind of departmental structure. If the subsequent moves mentioned above take place,
the net reduction in the number of departments since end-1966 will
have been ten. Two saved in the overseas field by the merging of
Commonwealth Office and then Overseas Development with the
Foreign Office ; one by the DHSS merger ; Aviation and the Post
Office ; three (Trade, Technology, Power) replaced by DTI ; four

(Transport, Housing & Local Government, Land and Natural Resources, Public Building & Works) by DOE. Instead of 19 (or 20) we have nine or ten.

Each of these departments must have the capability to decide issues within its own bailiwick, to formulate its objectives and priorities, to develop its long-term expenditure programme and to carry it out, and to plan its own civil service manpower. There is no inherent difficulty in this. It is a question of organisation and of getting the right staff into the right position rather than a matter of new specialisation and esoteric techniques. Within two or three years one would expect every one of them to have as much of this capability as it needs.

In these central matters the departments depend upon the agreement of the Prime Minister and sometimes the Cabinet on issues of political importance, and on the approval of the Treasury and the Civil Service Department. But the nature of these constraints from the centre should change as a result of the changes in the number, size and structure of departments. If it did not do so, indeed, one important purpose of the creation of 'giant' departments and the establishment of effective systems for determining objectives and priorities and allocations would be lost.

Organisation at the Centre

We are here concerned with the shaping of the centre of the machinery of government—the Cabinet at the political level, and the Cabinet Office, the Treasury and the Civil Service Department at the official level. We are concerned both with the structure and the method of operation at the centre in itself, and the relationship between the centre and the nine major departments.

Size of the Cabinet

Beginning with the political side, the size of the Cabinet begins to decide itself. It will become a practical minimum of sixteen :
  Prime Minister
  Lord President
  Chancellor of the Exchequer
  Lord Privy Seal (Civil Service Department)
  Lord Chancellor
  Nine Departmental Ministers
  Scotland
  Wales

Prime Ministers may find it necessary or desirable to bring in more (at present, for instance, Mr Rippon, the Chancellor of the Duchy of Lancaster). There will be a number of Ministers outside the Cabinet carrying an equivalent pay and rank (notably the No 2s in the 'giant' departments) ; but it would seem unlikely that there will in future be any (such as previous Ministers of Power or Health) who might sometimes be in the Cabinet and sometimes out. From the point of view of the proper conduct of public business, the concept of a departmental Minister outside the Cabinet was never a good one. Such a Minister was at a great disadvantage (irrationally from the point of view of the relative importance of his and other Ministers' work) when bringing his business to the Cabinet ; so the disappearance of such Ministers would be welcome. A future Prime Minister may, of course, change the departmental structure, and with it the Cabinet structure. But the advantages of stability of departmental structure have been emphasised, and are much greater with ten departments than with twenty ; and the element of stability of Cabinet structure which would flow from this has much to commend it.

Provided that the system of the 'giant' departments works well, there is no *prima facie* reason why a government with a different economic and social philosophy should require a different departmental structure, unless the differences of philosophy were so great that they could not be accommodated within our present structure of government and administration. To any government the cost of a further great series of changes in departmental structure should be very daunting.

Cabinet Decision-Making

By 'the Cabinet' here I mean the collective decision-making apparatus of Ministers, the Cabinet and its ministerial committees. This is a group of men and women of whom say 16–20 are Cabinet members and another 25 or so participate in the committee structure. They are people of diverse talents and backgrounds, mostly with considerable experience of political life, but, in the nature of things few will have knowledge in depth of the subject for which their departments are responsible.

It is sometimes thought that there is a close analogy between the decision-making in Cabinet and the decision-making of the board of directors of a company or any other executive group. There are certain common strands running through all committee work, but this analogy cannot be pressed very far. The width of the business of the Cabinet, with the only link between its various parts being politics and the responsibility to govern ; the clamant pressure from events outside to take decisions, often with little time and altogether inadequate information ; the intolerable load of business and activity upon every Cabinet Minister, and his dual responsibility both for his own department and his share in the Cabinet's decisions ; the fact that most decisions must be announced immediately, and become the subject of public debate and criticism after publication, the fact that it is only rarely possible to explain the full reasons for the decision ; the insecurity of the personal positions of the Ministers themselves, with never an assurance of more than five years' office (and that only very occasionally), and the continuous risk of sudden disappearance from the scene, often for quite unforeseeable and indeed irrational reasons.

Admittedly, if a great business organisation had to be run like this at the top, the results might be odd ; but if these characteristics of Cabinet government were replaced by a system more like that of industry at the top, other kinds of difficulties would follow. The essential elements of Cabinet government must be taken as they are. On the other hand, it is clear that these special characteristics can lead to very bad decisions, and sometimes to avoidably bad decisions, and to reduce the incidence of these is one of the big machinery-of-government tasks. It follows that in setting up the organisation at the centre and the relation between the centre and the departments, we need specifically to try to eliminate the weaknesses in the system as they now appear.

In the problems which confront government, it is the political component (and not the technical component) which is decisive ; and this is the component which the Cabinet is uniquely fitted to decide. The natural way to express this is as a direction or indication of the kind of action called for, and not as a technical decision in depth. It is the mass of technical decision-making which overloads the Cabinet and leaves them no time to consider the strategy of their policies or to clarify their political objectives.

So the purpose must surely be to have machinery which seeks to bring about a situation in which every member of the Cabinet is well equipped to take political decisions over the immense width of affairs the Cabinet has to deal with and within the instant time-scales involved— and by 'political' I mean the objectives, the value-judgments, the view of what public opinion will or will not stand—but leave the technical decision in depth to the departmental ministers. There is no clear-cut line which divides 'political' from 'technical' ; but there is certainly a spectrum, and the great reduction in the number of departments should make it easier to move along this spectrum in the required direction. This is the heart of the matter; and the swamping of Cabinet business by questions for 'technical' decision—whether economic, industrial, diplomatic, social service, environmental—at the expense of 'political' decisions may well have been one of the main reasons why our governmental performance has appeared to have worked badly in the last decades.

Functions in the Centre

The departmental structure at the centre is a combination of the Cabinet Office, the Treasury and the Civil Service Department (CSD). These three organisations, whose official heads hold the three top posts in the Home Civil Service, live very closely together, and although their interrelationships change over the years, according to different Prime Ministers and Chancellors of the Exchequer and the differing personalities at the top, it makes most sense to think of them as one group.

The functions are best considered not in terms of the units in the centre (which are intrinsically one group) but in terms of the related tasks, whichever unit does them. There is the self-contained central work— the Cabinet secretariat (with a co-ordinating role e.g. in defence and overseas policy) ; CSD's work in advising the Prime Minister on the machinery of government ; and its responsibility for the civil service (pay, recruitment, structure, training, Civil Service College, etc). Then there is the Treasury's work on the management of the national economy, on home and overseas finance, and, with the revenue departments, on fiscal policy : and its role in the co-ordination of economic policy. In each of these cases, the Treasury or the CSD or the Cabinet Office is the responsible department for doing the work, and draws on other departments for whatever help it needs, but in the end it must decide itself.

Centre and Departments

The functions of the centre in relation to departments are entirely different. There is the central work on the department's objectives and priorities or Programme Analysis Review (PAR) and the analysis of issues for the Cabinet—done by Lord Rothschild's Central Policy Review Staff (CPRS) and the Treasury. There is public expenditure allocation (Public Expenditure Survey Committee, or PESC) and control—done by the Treasury's public sector divisions. There is the control of departments' staff numbers and manpower and organisation, senior appointments, management services—done by CSD.

Here the centre is dealing with the work of the departments, for which the departmental Ministers are responsible. Decisions must be taken which determine the constraints of money or manpower or other resources within which each department must work : these constraints must be determined by the Cabinet ; and this is a joint process for the centre and the departments. After the constraints have been laid down, the centre must make sure that the departments comply with them : this, too, is a joint operation. Again, there may be disputes or incompatibilities between departments, and these have to be sorted out, by the centre and the departments together. The nature of the relationship between the centre and the departments is the crux of the ability of the whole governmental machine to work smoothly and effectively.

The relationship, as the Plowden Report on the Control of Public Expenditure said,
    'should be one of joint working together in a common enterprise :

41

it should be considered not in terms of more or less "independence" of the departments from "control" by the Treasury [and Civil Service Department], but rather in terms of getting the right balance and differentiation of function.'[1]

With nine or ten large departments, all powerfully equipped to deal with their objectives, priorities, expenditure programmes and manpower, the nature of this relationship will inevitably become very different —notably in scale and detail of contacts and degree of supervision—from what it had been when there were twenty departments without such equipment.

We must note at once that there is potentially an issue of organisation at the centre, for parts of the Treasury, CSD and Cabinet Office (notably CPRS) are engaged on this joint work with only nine or ten departments; and this is potentially a source of friction. Before 1964, only one department—the Treasury—was concerned in this role; and although it is true that the two sides of the Treasury worked not much more closely together than the Treasury and CSD do now, there was only one Minister in charge of both, and there was geographical contiguity, which will not remain. Seven years ago, there was one department in the centre and 19/20 operating departments. Now there are three units in the centre and 9/10 operating departments, which is a most remarkable change.

The PAR-PESC Operations

Before going into the implications of this, however, we must consider the substance of the relationships, and the practical tasks to be done. PAR and PESC should be seen as one very large operation, consisting of a number of stages, designed to enable the government to:

(a) create an overall strategy across the whole range of those of its policies which involve significant use of resources.

(b) establish the objective of each department and the priorities between them, considered over a five-year period, and in particular to determine which are the marginal objectives, affected by small changes up or down in the resources allocated to the department.

(c) determine the allocations between the departments, and so provide the resource framework within which each department can work.

(d) ensure that departments keep within their allocations, both of money and of civil service manpower.

(e) have an effective means of making day-to-day decisions within this framework of overall strategies, departmental objectives and priorities, and departmental allocations.

PAR and PESC are designed to become the basis of a new system of formulating and carrying out the government's policy. This should not

[1] Cmnd 1432 of July 1961, para 34.

be regarded as an addition to the conventional system : for if it survives it must ultimately replace the traditional system, and will be the system of expenditure and manpower administration and control within the departments, at the centre, and between the two. There cannot be two methods by which the thousands of decisions about spending and staff are taken, both operating simultaneously. In a transition period, elements of the old and new systems will be going on at the same time. But it is to everybody's interest to get through the transition quickly ; and what is said here is aimed at the end of the transition period, two to five years ahead.

I must emphasise that in these lectures I am trying to look to the time when the PAR-PESC system is in full operation some years ahead, to see how it will work and what its implications will be. I am not trying to describe what PAR and PESC are now. PAR is in the experimental introduction phase ; and PESC is still being continuously adapted in the light of experience and new needs ; and it is necessary to proceed in this way. I am talking about how the future PAR and PESC could, and in my opinion should, be shaped in order to provide a politically and administratively effective system for carrying out the objectives which have been laid down. I think this is how they will develop, but that is only my own opinion. To avoid any misunderstanding, I will refer to my future concept of PAR as PAR(O) and of PESC as PESC(O). When I refer to them without the 'O', I am talking about the generally accepted doctrines and procedures in March 1971.

The Departments' PAR(O) Returns

We start with nine operating departments—FCO, Defence (including any future defence procurement body), DTI, DOE, DHSS, DES, Home Office, MAFF, Employment. It is important to recognise that the operation could not be effectively carried out with 20 departments. The essence of PAR is that a large number of individuals (Cabinet Ministers and the officials in the centre) must understand the programmes of all departments and relate them to each other and compare them. This may be just possible with nine returns—though six would be much better. It becomes utterly impossible when one gets into higher figures, for no one can comprehend so many programmes. It follows that the minor units must be dealt with separately. It is accidental, but a fortunate accident, that the creation of 'giant' departments has led to a figure of nine which is about the maximum that in my opinion the PAR/PESC system can accommodate.

I assume that Scotland continues to be treated as now, so that the various departmental programmes (health, education, roads etc) are in effect handled on a 'Great Britain' basis and Scotland's (and Wales's) shares are decided afterwards. In my opinion it will probably ultimately become necessary to add the Treasury (with the revenue departments), for I would regard the taxation objectives and priorities as being indispensable in creating a realistic expenditure strategy.[2]

A separate programme on the edge of PAR/PESC is likely to be needed for nationalised industries' investment (subsidies, of course, come into the relevant departments' programmes). This expenditure is much more akin to private investment than to the general run of government expenditure; and although nationalised-industry investment is an important element in goverment strategy, the considerations and criteria which guide government policy here have little in common with those which govern expenditure on defence, education, roads etc. The electricity supply industry must be allowed to invest enough to meet the nation's future estimated power needs; and the airlines must be allowed to equip themselves to hold their own with their overseas competitors. The way in which they determine their needs and the ground rules determining their pricing and marketing policy must be laid down by the government. The estimated aggregate size of their investment is a factor in determining the tolerable size of future public expenditure, just as is the estimated future level of private investment. But one cannot really say that the steel industry's investment is any more directly competitive for resources with the education programme than is the chemical industry's investment: the nationalised industries' requirement for government finance is an essential part of the picture, but this is an entirely different concept from the physical investment.

The nine Departments (and the Treasury for taxation) would submit their PAR(O) returns to the centre. This would be a big descriptive paper, with an appendix showing expenditure figures five years ahead, implicit in the policies described. This pattern would be different for each department, but each would analyse by purpose (e.g. for education, primary, secondary, further and higher, distinguishing the requirements called for by inevitable increases in numbers from those for making improvements); would seek to establish yardsticks by which performance can be measured against programme; and would distinguish the areas which the department can control from those which it cannot. The figures (and thus the policies described) would be based upon the department's previous five-year allocations, with margins up and down, with the priorities for cutting and spending clearly spelt out.

The PAR(O) return would be annual, with specific areas selected by the CPRS for examination in depth. As the departments begin to have their policies formulated in this way, the change from year to year both in objectives and in priorities would become quite small. The process would be a useful discipline, requiring new ideas to have to find their

[2] Cf Sir Richard Clarke, *The Management of the Public Sector of the National Economy*, Stamp Memorial Lecture, 1964, page 24.

place in relation to existing ones ; and moderating the tendency to jump from one idea to another. After a change of government, the first PAR returns would be very important.

PAR(O) Decisions

After examination of the PAR return at the centre, by Treasury and CPRS and in some cases CSD, to check its internal consistency and to sort out any elements in it which would affect other departments' policies (not very many of these when there are nine departments, mostly well known and likely to be cleared beforehand), each PAR return would be considered by the Cabinet or a special Cabinet committee for the purpose (but one involving nearly everybody in a 16–17 Cabinet, for the spending Ministers must see all the other spending programmes and the taxation programme in order to carry out their dual role as departmental Minister and Cabinet Minister). If departmental Ministers are allowed to escape from collective responsibility for the whole, they will obviously behave as departmental Ministers, and not as Cabinet Ministers.

The purpose of the Cabinet examination would be to endorse (or amend) the direction of the Minister's policy and his objectives and priorities. This is an indispensable preparation for PESC (the absence of which has been a serious disadvantage hitherto), as well as erecting a sound and agreed basis for government policy. A substantial meeting for each of ten PAR returns (and perhaps some time later to get the conclusion firm) may look heavy ; but one meeting a year to get the government's policy settled for each of these ten areas (subject to the marginal arithmetic of the subsequent PESC) is truly economical in time.

I must emphasise that the procedure is useless if the PAR returns show requirements which are far greater than the resources, for discussion at PAR would then become unrealistic, and if unachievable policies are approved, the subsequent PESC operation becomes a shambles. The provision that the returns should be consistent with the previous five years' allocation (with plus and minus tranches) is meant to look after this ; but it is not entirely unknown for allocations to be made, which in the light of a year's experience turn out to be hopelessly above what the taxation objective (and thus the economy as a whole) can tolerate. But the PAR system would make it difficult for a Minister and his department to live for long in a state of unreality.

PAR and PESC Timing

The PAR operation is the first stage of the full system outlined on p. 42. The timing is important. In the developed system, with each department doing its annual PAR, it will be impossible for these to be completed, examined and submitted to Ministers in one simultaneous operation.

It would probably take the Cabinet five or six months to give the required consideration to the ten departments' returns. So the idea of getting all the PAR's neatly completed and then proceeding to the PESC allocation will never in my opinion be practicable.

The PESC operation must, of course, be simultaneous. Some departments will be working on current PAR decisions and some on last year's. The departments' PAR time tables could be arranged so that the most important would be 'current' at the time of PESC. It is simplest, perhaps, to look at PAR as establishing the strategy for individual departments, steadily revised over time, and PESC as taking the tactical decision for everybody once a year.

PESC(O) Preparation

The great reduction in the number of departments, coupled with the existence of PAR returns (including one on taxation) agreed by the Cabinet, would make the annual PESC operation much easier. In my view, as one who has been very closely connected with this from the start, the idea of PAR was always implicit in the concepts of PESC, and when it was developed by Mr Meyjes and Mr East it seemed to me clearly right. In retrospect one can see that some of the deficiencies experienced in the working of PESC may be attributable in some degree to the absence of PAR.

The first step in PESC(O) would be the consideration of the 'medium-term economic assessment' report produced by the centre, setting out the prospects for the national economy as a whole for five years ahead, and expressing the relationship between taxes and public expenditure for the same period. This would establish the basis for the argument between the relative desirability of lower taxes (in terms of the priorities in the 'taxation' PAR decisions) and higher expenditures, which would be considered on the basis of a taxation strategy proposal by the Chancellor of the Exchequer; and then between the nine programmes of departmental expenditure.

Ground rules would be laid down for the differing treatment of different economic categories of expenditure, as some types of expenditures are of the nature of investments, yielding an economic return to the national economy, and others not. These forms of analysis are not yet far developed. It is clear, for example, that there is a tangible economic return on road building, and very little (in this sense) on pensions; and that the former is a direct charge on resources while the latter is an indirect charge (as the pension is spent). But we are far from clear in showing how these considerations should be weighed against one another.

The 'medium-term assessment' would require to be discussed by the

Cabinet (or the special Cabinet committee) just as the PAR returns had been ; for only by this means can departmental Ministers reach the understanding of the situation that enables them to carry out their Cabinet Minister role as well as that of departmental Minister. When the chairmen of the subsidiaries of a great holding company join the board, each has to handle the work of his subsidiary and press its claims for resources on the board while at the same time appraising the over-riding interest of the holding company : and this dual appreciation is indispensable.

PESC(O) Allocation

The scene is then set for the allocation decision. The Cabinet will have had its previous discussion and decisions on each of the nine PAR(O) and the 'taxation' PAR(O) ; and it will be informed of the relationship between the tax marginal movements (up and down) and the public expenditure marginal movements (up and down) resulting from the discussion of the medium-term economic assessment ; and have the Chancellor's proposal on where the line should be drawn between taxation and expenditure. With this Cabinet background of full know-ledge and discussion, the officials in the centre will be able to prepare sharp and straightforward papers analysing the alternatives. Five-year expenditure allocations (with a descending degree of firmness year by year) and taxation blueprints could be determined without undue difficulty. Indeed, by being better prepared to take their decisions, the Cabinet might well be able to make good some of the extra time which they had spent on the PAR returns.

Each department would thus have its resources allocation in practical terms ; and as a by-product the civil service manpower allocation for each. It would certainly not be sensible to try to do a civil service manpower allocation by a separate process of collection of returns from departments.

Implementing the Decisions

The outcome is a series of nine public expenditure allocations for a period of five years with descending firmness, rolled forward by one year in each year's operation, together with some suitable limit for civil service manpower. The 'public expenditure' is, of course, a different concept from government expenditure. Broadly speaking, it includes all expenditure by the department (current and capital), all expenditure by local authority (current and capital) in the department's field, and the gross expenditure of the National Insurance Funds. For some of the departments much consists of expenditure over which the department has no formal control at all (particularly DES and DOE) ; and within the direct government expenditure, the amount over which the department has no effective control (for the amounts paid out are determined by the number of applicants who are entitled to the money under the law) is substantial. Again, the concept of a five-year period introduces a new dimension into government finance; and the concept of an allocation of £X million at constant prices is elusive.

The procedure and the decisions are useless without a lucid and effective system for implementing them. Here is the greatest weakness in the present PESC system; and refinement is futile without the implementation system. This leads straight into the system of central financial and manpower control, i.e. the way in which departments manage their own spending and manpower, and the way in which the Treasury and the Civil Service Department manage the departments.

Departments' Commitments

The decisions determining expenditure allocations cannot be said to commit the departments in any accounting sense of the term. If the departments do not themselves incur the expenditure, or are simply agents in paying out money to companies or to individuals in statutory schemes, they obviously cannot enter into such commitments. The decisions are neither 'rations' which entitle the department to the use of a certain amount of resources; nor are they like the conventional Estimates figures which express the state of an argument between the department and the Treasury about how much money the department would need, with the department able to ask for a Supplementary Estimate if the figure turns out too low, and surrendering the excess if the figure turns out to be too high.

If the system is to be viable, Cabinet decisions should, in my opinion, commit the departments to do their best, both in their own spending and in influencing that of local authorities, to keep the expenditure within the allocation; and to plan their forward policy on this basis. This is the basis upon which the department's work should be founded; and not, as it were, the automatic consequence of policies already laid down. The whole PAR/PESC system implies this. But the concept is not yet sharp enough to permit departments and the Treasury to handle this as the effective tool of financial operation. The conduct of expenditure business is an eternal dialogue between the department and the Treasury; and if the PESC allocation is the heart of it, as it must be, both sides must know exactly and precisely how they are going to work it.

Department—Treasury Concordat

For this purpose, a formal concordat between each department and the Treasury is essential, to lay down precisely how both are going to work. This must be carefully and precisely negotiated, for in a giant department large numbers of people are involved. In July 1968, 'second Mintech' agreed such a concordat with the Treasury. The experience both of negotiating this and of working it underlined the deep problems involved in setting up a financial system which puts the pressures in the right places and concentrates everybody's attention on the relevant points.

The right way to do this, in my opinion, is to break down the department's total expenditure in a manner that makes it possible to get sharper commitments in those areas which the department can control, and a more explicit statement of what it will do in those areas where it does not control. This develops a strategy for dealing with the whole of the expenditure. If the Treasury is satisfied with the strategy and with the department's internal procedures for giving effect to it, the corollary is that the need for Treasury control over the department's day-to-day transactions disappears. In other words, the 'concordat' sets out the department's expenditure planning and control system by which it intends to 'do its best' to keep within its allocation; and the extent to which the activities of the department under this system will need to be supervised by the Treasury.

Categories of Expenditure

The right way to group the department's expenditures for this purpose is in terms of financial control systems, for example :

I   Expenditures reasonably within the department's control, and which can be programmed ahead.
II Expenditures by the department of a nature that cannot be programmed ahead, because one cannot know what demands will arise and what they will cost.
III Expenditures by the department under legislation, which cannot be altered except by changing the law.
IV Expenditure by local authorities and other bodies outside the department's direct financial control.

The expenditures in Category I should all be included in a ration—a total figure, projected ahead as appropriate, with specific rules about how it is changed from year to year. The department undertakes to keep within this ration; and the proper course is for expenditure within this ration to be totally free from Treasury control. There will be a full review each year when the 'ration' is negotiated : the department could provide every three months a list of commitments entered into, reconciling this with the ration; and the Treasury could select say two or three cases in each of these quarterly records to examine what has happened and to satisfy itself that the system is effectively worked. The Mintech arrangements with the Treasury provided for a Category I of this kind : with large freedom, though not the full freedom which in my view is essential to give the giant department the responsibility and width of action that it must have and to eliminate correspondence and discussion about trivia.[3]

The expenditures in Category II are more difficult to deal with. If their needs cannot be predicted five years ahead, it is clearly unrealistic to try to establish a 'ration' : it is unrealistic from the point of view of the department, for if the department does not know whether the requirement will be £X or £2X, it cannot properly undertake to keep within £X ; and it is unrealistic from the point of view of the Treasury, for the true requirement might just as easily be £$\frac{1}{2}$X and to concede a ration of £X would be giving the department resources unnecessarily. For example, in the late 1960s the Concorde programme was costing about £50 million a year : if it had been a failure and had had to be cancelled, there would have been no justification for the Ministry of Technology to be allowed to spend the £50 million a year on something else, as would have been the case if this programme had been included in a 'ration' like Category I. Nor would it have been sensible to have made the provision of £42 million for the Rolls Royce RB 211–22 engine conditional upon the department reducing its other programmes by £42 million as would have been the case if this sort of expenditure was handled as part of a 'ration'.

Expenditures in Category II therefore must be handled *ad hoc* between the department and the Treasury. The overall allocation to the department must provide for this. The provision will depend upon the policy of the government and the expectation that expenditures will in fact have to be incurred but this cannot be expressed as a 'ration', and there can be no presumption either that the department would be 'entitled' to bring forward proposals up to that amount or that it would be debarred from bringing forward proposals costing more.[4] Category II should only include large items : small items of this kind can, of course, be fitted into the large 'ration' in Category I.

The expenditures in Category III are straightforward, though often very difficult to predict—the future cost of the agricultural price guarantees which depend upon the level of market prices and the size of the output, and the future cost of social security benefits, are examples. Here again, the idea of a 'ration' is irrelevant, for if the department has an open-ended statutory commitment it must honour it continuously. Likewise there is no need for Treasury control of the administration of such

[3] Our Category I was a large chunk of civil expenditures—cost of our research establishments and AEA Civil R & D ; grants to industrial research associations ; development contracts for industry ; advances to NRDC ; support for British Standards Institution and Metrication Board ; National Computing Centre ; regional advisory services ; pre-production orders for machine tools ; hovercraft ; oceanography ; and of course HQ expenditure etc, running at about £100 million a year. Operating these within a 'ration' forced us to assess this variety of expenditures against one another.
[4] In Mintech, Category II included the civil aircraft launching aid projects, international space projects, Shipbuilding Industry Board and other shipbuilding and industrial reorganisation projects, advances to IRC etc.

legislation, except, of course, to the extent that changes of the method of administration alter the cost by more than an agreed figure.[5]

For Category IV, where the expenditure is not within the direct control of the department, e.g. local authority expenditure, the essential element is a process of discussion between the department and the Treasury to consider how the expenditure can be contained by indirect means, or, indeed, perhaps by changes in the law. The local authorities are responsible for about 25% of total public expenditure (as defined in PESC) ; and one cannot talk seriously about establishing objectives and priorities and allocation of resources without incorporating the 25% into the system.

These expenditures and the policies related to them are handled in the PAR/PESC returns mainly for DOE and DES.[6] But when the allocations have been made, neither DOE nor DES (nor the other departments with local government services) have power to control the expenditure to keep it within the allocation. They can affect the expenditure by specific departmental actions, either by applying nation-wide changes (e.g. in payments for school meals) or by applying existing controls of local authority expenditure (e.g. on the capital side). The government can apply pressure to the local authorities by reducing the rate support grant, increasing the area of marginal expenditure which has to be met entirely from the rates and other local authority income. But this does not distinguish between, e.g. education and health (and thus logically credit or debit to DES's or DHSS's allocation) : and some authorities will prefer to go on expanding their expenditure and so frustrate the government's fiscal objective. Much can be done on these lines, but the scope for straightforward national changes is now small (and tends to be at the periphery of policy).

The problem of getting the right kind of articulation between central government and local authorities in the development of expenditure programmes will become very important in the coming years, particularly as many of the fastest expanding programmes (roads, law and order, miscellaneous local services, education) are predominantly those undertaken by local authorities. This is obviously closely linked with local government reform. It is certainly one of the most important aspects of local government reform ; and it is also one of the most fundamental aspects of a successful PAR-PESC public expenditure management.

[5] The Mintech illustrations in this category were investment grants and the loans and grants under the Local Employment Acts.

[6] Great Britain local authorities current and capital expenditure in 1971–72 £5,335 million, of which education £2,251 million, housing, roads, transport, miscellaneous local services £2,157 million, law and order £576 million, health and welfare £302 million. *Public Expenditure 1969–70 to 1974–75*, Cmnd 4578, Page 50.

Form of 'Concordat'

The nature of the 'concordat' between the department and the Treasury described above is thus becoming clear. It would start from the five-year allocation for the department as laid down in the Cabinet's decisions and define how these will be changed from year to year, and the circumstances in which they can be changed at other times (e.g. demands by the Treasury for short-term cuts on grounds of national economic emergency; or demands by the department for additional allocation to meet some new large and unexpected requirement). It would define Categories I, II, III and IV in detail. It would determine the 'ration' for Category I, and the rules governing it, and the removal of 'Treasury control' within the category, and the arrangements for quarterly statements of commitments made and reconciliation with the ration, and provision for *ex post facto* checks. It would determine the 'estimated spend' included in the total allocation separately for Categories II, III and IV, and the minimum provisions for Treasury control under each.

But perhaps most important of all, for the time-scales of most government expenditures extend far beyond the normal spans of individual Ministers and the individual officials in specified jobs both in the department and in the Treasury, is the objective which both will seek to achieve. To carry out the economic objective of keeping within the allocation and planning the department's whole business on this basis, the first step after the allocation is decided must be a statement by the department of how it intends to operate in order to do this, and for agreement to be reached with the Treasury on it. Category I is straight-forward when the 'ration' is fixed : in Category II, there is nothing to be done but await developments : but in Category III and Category IV there are real issues of strategy, on whether it is desirable to seek new arrangements, if necessary by new legislation, to limit the open-endedness of particular government commitments, or of seeking new means of getting *de facto* control over public expenditures outside the government's direct control.

The obverse of providing for this serious and continuing dialogue between the department and the Treasury on the strategic issues of the control of the department's public expenditure and setting up forces which will enable it to be contained within its allocation, is the virtual abandonment of Treasury control and censorship of the department's expenditure in detail. Such Treasury approvals are needed in Category II (but all these are by definition large issues of public policy). There may be cases in which standard practice between departments is so essential and so unattainable by general rule without looking at individual cases that some case-by-case approval may be needed. But the onus should be on the Treasury to prove the need for any prior approval of any item of expenditure.

New System of Expenditure Control

The system of public expenditure control which we are now approaching stands the traditional system on its head. The traditional system saw the expenditure of a department (and indeed the total expenditure of the departments) as the sum of thousands of individual items; and thus the essence of the control of expenditure was the control of the items. The control of the items was delegated by the Treasury to the departments, partly in chunks brought together in sub-heads to which the Treasury's control applied, and partly in items of more than a specific size, which had to be submitted for Treasury approval individually. The dialogue between the Treasury and the department was in terms of items, not in terms of totals. The system which is developing, on the other hand, sees its focal point in the total—i.e. in the allocation—and the subject of the dialogue is, at one time of the year (early in the PAR/PESC process) and at another time of the year (immediately after the PESC decision) concerned with the total size of the department's expenditure and how it can be kept within a certain level—with the onus entirely on the department to deal with the items accordingly.

The Treasury must be satisfied that the department handles both its detailed work and the total efficiently; but this is no justification in itself for the seldom constructive process of Treasury approval of individual items. The examination of the department's five-year programme for PAR and PESC; the breakdown of the department's expenditures and objectives on the post-PESC determination of the handling of Categories I–IV; the progress reports of commitments in Category I, and the individual cases in Category II and the strategy discussions in Categories III and IV; together with the arrangements for *ex post facto* consideration of selected individual cases—all this constitutes an intimate relationship between the department and the Treasury. Admittedly this will require a great deal of work and considerable and unfamiliar expertise. It will certainly inform the Treasury adequately of the way in which the department does its business; and enable the centre to take better decisions and make wiser proposals; and it will also inform the departments of the problems of the centre, and help them to make their own work more realistic and effective. In short, the new system will be much more constructive and relevant to the real problems of the management and control of public expenditure in the 1970s.

Civil Service Manpower

Everyone agrees that there should be fewer civil servants. Of course, the number actually depends upon the tasks that government imposes upon them. When we change from investment grants to investment allowances, this will eventually save 1,000 staff. Again, one cannot easily define 'civil servants' and count them meaningfully. The conventional definition excludes 'industrial workers' (200,000, and difficult to distinguish on the borderline from the 500,000 non-industrials) ; and excludes the staffs of government-financed bodies, such as the research councils, whose staffs do not differ at all from those employed in the departments' laboratories. Nevertheless, however dependent the numbers are on policy, and however irrational the definitions, a steady increase in numbers is troublesome in a stationary population ; and I would not want to argue against the most effective checks for preventing this growth.

The considerations about manpower control are similar to those about financial control from the centre. There should be an annual discussion between the department and the CSD to decide how much civil service manpower the department will need for the PESC period. The department undertakes to do its best to contain its manpower within this limit, and will plan its business accordingly. This having been agreed, alongside or as part of the PAR/PESC, it is left to the department to act accordingly, with a regular progress report to the CSD. As I said earlier a giant department must as an ordinary matter of management limit its man-power, whatever the centre may require, and there is no difficulty about this unless the control is taken to a point at which it becomes self-defeating.

The CSD still retains control of departments' complementing, inherited from the Treasury and analogous to the detailed financial controls. These equally need radical revision. There must be general conformity of practice between the departments in the number of posts at the top ; and the CSD must clearly approve every post at or above Under Secretary rank, i.e. the new senior policy and management group, which numbers 657. This control should also embrace the 279 posts between Under Secretary and Assistant Secretary level.

But I cannot see how the CSD can pass a sensible judgment on whether a giant department should or should not add another Assistant Secretary or Deputy Chief Scientific Officer post—290 at this level in 'last Mintech' ; or to the much larger numbers at the next row down, the Senior Principal Scientific Officers, for example. No one at the centre can possibly know a department well enough to 'approve' or 'disapprove' in such detail. To pretend to do this is a waste of everybody's time, and damages the credibility of the control from the centre. There are other minor CSD manpower controls ; and in this as in financial control, the onus should be put on the centre to prove the need for the control, not *vice versa*. It is necessary to standardise the conditions about employment across the service ; but this has been used too often as an excuse for detailed central control. It is an unfortunate truth, alas, that such control from the centre is not always as unwelcome as it should be to departments, for it is always easier internally to say 'I'm sorry I can't persuade the CSD to agree', than to say, 'No'. It is equally true that this kind of detailed censorship is much easier for the centre to carry out than the modern central function which I am expounding.

In manpower as in finance the traditional practice has been to see the work of Whitehall as a series of individual items, with control from the centre of some sets of items and of some of the most important items (i.e. the more senior complementing). Here, too, the traditional system is being turned on its head, with the giant department as the unit and the CSD's task being to establish the centre's constraints upon the department's freedom of action, and above all to satisfy itself that the department's organisation and system for handling its manpower problems is effective. Instead of thinking about whether a department with a staff of 25,000 should be entitled to employ 322 or 323 Senior Principal Scientific Officers the CSD's true task is to satisfy itself that such a department is efficient and to form a judgment whether the department's work could be done perfectly well with 24,000 instead of 25,000, or that with 26,000 it would be done disproportionately better. This needs a great deal of new and original thought.

Organisation Expertise

So the emphasis is changing from the approval of large numbers of details to the examination of control systems and organisation of giant departments. The question of senior appointments is closely linked with this. The Permanent and Deputy Secretary and equivalent posts are subject to the Prime Minister's approval on the recommendation of the Head of the Civil Service. To be capable of approving these appointments and their complementing at Under Secretary level and the inclusion of everybody at this level in a unified civil service top hamper really does require a detailed knowledge and appreciation of the structure of every department.

There is not yet enough capability at the centre to appraise critically the organisation and control systems of giant departments. There are individuals with good judgment and knowledge in this as in every field. But there is not enough systematic assembly of information about the departments' practice, or basis for comparative analysis, or indeed a standard strategy for examining these problems. The interest and expertise of the central departments will increasingly lie in the constructive and critical handling of the big numbers, both in economic resources and in civil service manpower, and in the provision of services, and in the appraisal of organisation.

There have been many strands in this direction in the post-war history of the Treasury, and detailed central control is a shadow of what it was. But in my opinion large changes will be required in the organisation and work of the central departments to bring into being the effective joint working of the centre with nine powerful departments; and the problems of developing the new methods of government are at least as much in the centre as in the departments.

Organisation at the Centre

We can now return to the questions of organisation at the centre, which I interrupted earlier in order to consider the substance of the likely future relations between the centre and the departments and thus of the work of the centre itself. The distribution of the top staff between Civil Service Department, Treasury and Cabinet Office at end-1970 was :[7]

	Under-Sec and above	Perm Sec	Dep Sec to Perm Sec	Under-Sec to Dep Sec
Civil Service Department	31	2	6	23
Treasury	32	3	9	20
Cabinet Office	19	3	6	10
	82	8	21	53

The departments at the centre have more very senior staff. DTI and DOE have more Under-Secretaries and equivalent than the three central organisations put together, but each has three Permanent Secretaries and 16–17 Deputy Secretaries compared with the centre's eight and 21 respectively. This, of course, follows inevitably from the nature of the work.

Experience has shown that this area is best organised into three separate units, each under a Permanent Secretary of top seniority—at present, Sir William Armstrong, Sir Burke Trend and Sir Douglas Allen. It is now agreed that the attempts to manage with two in 1947–1956[8], and with a different structure in 1956–1962, loaded the two too heavily ; having three, with two brigaded together as Joint Permanent Secretaries to the Treasury in 1962–1968 proved unsatisfactory also. The three-unit pattern is likely to continue to be the situation, for one cannot see any of the new developments lightening the load enough to make it possible to share it between two again.

The table shows eight of Permanent Secretary rank at the end of 1970. This has varied widely through the years. In the late 1940s and early

[7] From Annex 1, including all staffs at equivalent salary levels. Cabinet Office did not then include Lord Rothschild or the newly-recruited CPRS, but some already included will come within this staff. Figures for Inland Revenue and Customs and Excise are 35 : 2 : 7 : 26 across the table.

[8] Even with one in 1945–1946. The course of the arrangements since the end of the war is set out in Annex 4.

1950s there were six or seven. During the 1950s, this fell to three—
the joint heads of the Treasury (one of whom was Secretary to the
Cabinet) and one Second Secretary. This proved manifestly inadequate,
and was raised to five by the appointment of two more Second
Secretaries in 1960, and to six after the Treasury reorganisation of
autumn 1962. From then on, and through the DEA period and including
Sir Solly Zuckerman's appointment as Chief Scientific Adviser in 1966,
the figure was seven or eight. With Lord Rothschild's appointment, I
would expect the figure to be usually about eight in the early 1970s.
The variation between three and eight top level jobs at the centre,
in 25 years in which the functions and responsibilities at the centre
have been subject to only marginal change, is an interesting subject
for thought.

Distribution of Functions

I will recapitulate the functions in the terms of the discussion:

(1)   Cabinet secretariat—the normal Cabinet Office job, including
      some interdepartmental co-ordination.
(2)   Machinery of government.
(3)   Responsibility for the civil service.
(4)   Central work on departments' organisation, management and
      senior appointments.
      (2), (3) and (4) are all CSD functions. They are growing in size and
      importance, partly because they have been underadministered
      in the past, and partly because the methods of central control
      are changing from casework to examination of systems.
(5)   Analysis, allocation and control of departments' objectives,
      expenditure, and civil service manpower.
      This is the work of the Treasury Public Sector Divisions, the
      CSD Manpower Divisions and the Central Policy Review Staff.
      This will probably grow but with some change of balance between
      senior and junior staff.
(6)   National economy, finance, taxation—the normal work of the
      Treasury National Economy and Finance Divisions, with the
      Revenue Departments.

The problems arise at the interfaces between the centre and the
departments, which is (4) and (5). This now engages all three central
organisations; and I believe that there will be increasing pressure to
have only one interface with the departments on this kind of work.
Faced with nine strong departments, each able to handle its economic
resources and manpower as described earlier, I doubt whether it will
be practicable for the centre to continue to be split into three units, each
dealing individually with the departments. There is no such pressure
yet, for the giant departments have not yet developed their strength

and organisation, and PAR is only tentative and experimental, and CPRS in its infancy. But I am sure that unless it all goes very wrong, the fragmentation in the centre's relations with the departments will become a real issue for thought, perhaps in a year, perhaps in two years or more.

Divided Responsibilities

How serious is the case likely to be for bringing together into one organisation the units in the Treasury, the CSD and the Cabinet Office that handle the centre's responsibility for managing and leading and organising and implementing the choices between the departments' objectives and resources and manpower? I would expect the case to become persuasive. There is a familiar dilemma in machinery of government, however, that the price of removing one difficulty is usually to create another; so the strength of the case is really important to judge.

I would note four potential sources of difficulty:

  (i) Departments greatly dislike having three separate contacts at the centre for closely related purposes; apart from the tiresomeness, it complicates their own organisation;

 (ii) Overlap in the handling of the PAR-PESC operation between the Treasury (and CSD) and CPRS;

(iii) Overlap and underlap between public expenditure control within the Treasury's and CSD's responsibility;

(iv) The essential role of management and organisation in all questions of control from the centre.

Overlap in PAR-PESC

The functions of CPRS[9] are bound to overlap those of the Public Sector Divisions of the Treasury. The staff will be composed of people some of whom will have different backgrounds from those who are doing the work in the Treasury, and their orientation will be different; but they will be performing the same function, which is to examine, question, analyse and relate together policy memoranda and projections of finance and resources; and to consider the inner consistency of each department's submission and its relation to the whole of public expenditure and the national economy. They will be doing some things that the Treasury does not do; and there are very good reasons for attaching them to the Cabinet Office and not to the Treasury, so that they can keep their different orientation. But the job in PAR-PESC operations is the same, and cannot be handled in duplicate with the departments without creating confusion in the centre and waste of time and frustration for departments.

[9] *The Reorganisation of Central Government.* Cmnd 4506. Paras 46–48.

58

One may hope and expect that the Treasury and CPRS will work together and will not indulge in separate dialogues with the departments. But inevitably they will sometimes draw different conclusions, and will want to advise Ministers differently. This could create a dangerous rift in the centre. In public expenditure policy this should always be avoided, not because public expenditure is more important than foreign policy or defence or taxation—for it is not—but because a clash at the centre on public expenditure engages the discipline and viability of the relation between the centre and the departments, and threatens the authority of the centre and the control of public expenditure itself. When the history of the management and control of public expenditure in the post-war decades comes to be written, the resignation of Mr Thorneycroft and his Financial and Economic Secretaries in January 1958 may well become identified as a watershed.

This problem will always arise if anyone in the centre is asked to carry out functions which overlap the Treasury's in the control of public expenditure. This does not matter in respect of the Treasury's other functions, for there the Chancellor of the Exchequer is carrying out a departmental responsibility like any other Minister, and this may have to be co-ordinated by somebody else with other Ministers' policies. But in public expenditure, the Chancellor has the central co-ordinating role, and is responsible for the management from the centre; and one cannot set up somebody else at the centre to co-ordinate the activities of the co-ordinator with those of the co-ordinated. The Cabinet Office has long been the co-ordinator of defence and overseas policy. It is now the co-ordinator for the Whitehall end of the Common Market negotiations.[10] But these are areas in which the public expenditure aspect is either not intrinsically dominant or (as in defence) is so dominant that the whole discussion starts from a Cabinet decision or assumption about it.

Over/Underlap between Treasury and CSD

When the Treasury and CSD were separated in 1968, it was decided that the Minister in charge of CSD would be responsible for approving departments' expenditure on staff and related costs; and that the

[10] The Cabinet Office is adopting this role formally for the first time. In the first Common Market negotiations of 1961–63 the Treasury was in the lead in the interdepartmental committee in Whitehall; likewise in the European free trade area negotiations of 1956–58; likewise in the NATO mutual aid negotiations in the early 1950s; and likewise again in the negotiations for the Marshall Plan and for the formation and development of OEEC in 1947 onwards. But the chairman and his staff in each case, though sitting in the Treasury, were regarded as non-departmental; and the Treasury's overseas financial interest was represented separately on the committees and in the negotiating teams. (The Treasury's public expenditure interest is not engaged.) The management could as easily have been Cabinet Office management as this kind of Treasury non-departmental management, although the latter had advantages at the time.

Treasury would not be involved. The cost of civil service pay is only about 9% of total Supply expenditure (and a much smaller proportion of PESC expenditure) : and it was recognised that any department's need for civil service manpower will usually follow its spending services, which must be approved by the Treasury. So the arrangement seemed manageable enough : indeed, it was much the same arrangement as existed between the two sides of the Treasury before.

But this does not necessarily make sense where civil service manpower is a large part of the cost of a department's work. The Revenue Departments spend over £130 million a year on civil service manpower. The issue is one of money, not manpower. How much administrative expenditure is worth incurring in order to collect more revenue? Should you spend an extra £X to collect an extra £Y? This is just the same problem as settling the procedures for claim checking or case investigation in the Department of Health and Social Security, or deciding how much to spend on the Ministry of Aviation Supply Contracts Division, or whether to work a testing facility at a research establishment round the clock in order to get more business. These are not issues of manpower control at all, unless manpower and finance are regarded as the same thing.

Again, the issues in government science research policy are mixed up between Treasury and CSD, with the Chief Scientific Adviser much involved too. Should the work be done with civil service manpower in government establishments, or in government-financed establishments whose staff does not count as 'civil service' (such as Atomic Energy Authority or research councils), or on contract to industry? Different manpower constraints are applied in these cases, but the money is the same. When DTI and DOE work out their research policies, they have to discuss them with three units in the centre and in three different manpower policy environments and ground rules. So it is very difficult to think lucidly on this difficult subject.

There is mistiness also in the responsibility for the wider public service questions. About 35% of Supply expenditure consists of pay etc. for the civil service, armed forces, doctors and nurses and others in the National Health Service, and the pay content of grants to local authorities (teachers, police, etc) and universities. The development of these services depend upon the growth and quality of their staff, which in turn depend considerably upon their pay. The responsibility for guiding the operating departments (DES, DHSS, Home Office, etc) is shared between Treasury and CSD (with the Department of Employment). There is less duplication here than underlap, for example :

(i) the pay problem (e.g. in the National Health Service) not brought clearly enough into relation with the numbers of staff and future growth of the service ;

(ii) the partial separation of pay from public expenditure considera-
      tions may encourage those engaged in public expenditure work
      to think in terms of 'expenditure at constant prices'—the built-in
      inflation concept that 'pay increases don't count';

(iii) neither Treasury nor CSD devote enough staff to public service
      manpower and pay work to make a real contribution to these
      most intractable problems: whatever one's view about government
      incomes policy for the private sector, the government must have
      a public service incomes policy, for here they are responsible
      either as employers or as providers of the money.

Many of us in the Treasury saw this split of responsibility for public
expenditure as a troublesome consequence of the creation of a separate
Civil Service Department, especially as the existence of this problem
did not seem to have been given weight by the Fulton Committee.
There were good arguments for separating the Civil Service Department
from the Treasury; and I would not argue that the expenditure argument
was overriding. But it left a problem which has not been solved. At the
beginning, the fact that the same staffs were doing the same jobs in the
same offices as before, and could be expected to co-operate as before
helped to reduce the problem; and in any case co-operation within
the old Treasury had been less close than one would now think necessary,
so potential rather than achieved gain was lost. But these offsets
diminish as the staffs change and the premises are moved; and the
problem is truly there.

Organisation and Management

Lastly and perhaps most importantly, the problems of public expenditure
control should increasingly be seen in terms of organisation and
management; and a major part of the Treasury's duty is to satisfy
itself that a department's system of financial decision-making and
administration is sound and properly manned. But there cannot be
two central sources of expertise about organisation, CSD and Treasury.
So either the Treasury will not do its proper job, or the Treasury and the
CSD must work so closely together that they are in effect one department.

A practical illustration is given by responsibility for investment grants.
This came to Mintech from the Board of Trade in October 1969 at
a moment that happened to be one of great concern, with expenditure
escalating above forecasts and much parliamentary investigation and
criticism. The only questions worth asking were, how good was the
procedure and organisation for making forecasts? Was the regional
organisation, which was paying out about £600 million a year with
1,000 staff at an annual cost of £2 million—a remarkably cheap operation—good enough: was it being done too much on the cheap? (In

fact it wasn't.) Our enquiry into this was halted by the decision to abandon the investment grant system, so the point turned out to be of only historical interest. But my point is that this was an immense money issue, which could be tackled only in organisation and management terms. But CSD was not in the operation ; and, indeed, it could have been awkward with CSD if we had found (which we did not) that substantially more staff were needed.

Scope for Reorganisation

So we have the frustration of the departments in having to deal with three central units on related questions, the potential or actual duplication between the three central units, and the fact that there can be only one source of expertise in the all-pervasive problem of organisation and management. I think there is a *prima facie* case for thinking about bringing them together at some future stage, when the new systems are established. It may be said, of course, that the three units will get on fine together and that these apprehensions are unnecessary. But if the three central units prove themselves to be so well-integrated and co-ordinated that, in practice they act as one, they had better be one, for this is much easier for everybody than a co-ordination effort. If they turn out to be unarticulated and to adopt different attitudes, the centre will become weak, and the government will be in trouble. If the departments are going to be as strong as is now planned, the centre must be strong enough to do its part.

I will outline two possible alternative forms of organisation, both of which bring together the three central units and the whole operation of the centre *vis-à-vis* the departments, and would remove the difficulties and anomalies that we have been discussing. All current management practice, in industry and everywhere else, agrees in bringing together the basic management of men and resources, and, of course, the determination of objectives, priorities and strategy. I stressed this in the chapter on the giant departments, and it must be true for the centre also.

However, in machinery of government the onus must always be on those who favour a change to demonstrate that there will not only be a balance of advantage in making a change, but that this will outweigh the disturbance cost throughout the system ; and although I am sure that we shall find the present system too weak and too fragmented at the centre, it is much too early to draw conclusions about whether there should be a change in two or three years' time, or what that change should be.

Federation at the Centre

One line of approach would be to bring together the whole lot into one organisation—Treasury, CSD, and the Central Policy Review Staff, everything except the Cabinet secretariat. This organisation could be constructed to provide a single interface with the departments in crucial areas, with the other functions in other parts of the organisation.

This could not be a giant unitary department on the lines that we have been considering. Adding the present organisations together, there would be, say, seven Permanent Secretaries (this number could no doubt come down to six or even five, but still a large number) plus the two heads of the Revenue Departments; and probably over 100 of Under-Secretary or above, including the Revenue Departments; and this is too big for a unitary department. Nor would I see advantage in trying to construct a double-headed department, like the Treasury from 1956 to 1968, or a treble-headed department, like the Treasury from 1916 to 1919. At first sight, the kind of organisation that we are thinking about here would be like the Treasury of the early 1960s, but leaving aside the question whether it is ever sensible to try to go back to former machineries of government, the expansion of what one may call the 'Civil Service Department' work and the introduction of PAR add further dimensions to what was already a very heavily loaded organisation.

This leads to the idea of a federal structure, with three or even more sub-departments linked only by a small superstructure. The three might be Management, Public Sector, and National Economy & Finance[11]. They would be largely independent, with cross-links in related subjects, and with interchangeable staff and common seniority and promotion procedures. Each would have its own Permanent Secretary, and some might have two. There would be a single Permanent Secretary of the whole department, the Head of the Civil Service, who would have some co-ordinating functions; but he would not be running the department like the head of a giant department, with the key management and budget divisions under his own supervision.

This federal system would be akin to the system set up in the Treasury reorganisation of October 1919[12]. This was imposed by the Finance Committee of the Cabinet, and was worked out by Lord Milner. Sir Warren Fisher was brought in from the Inland Revenue to become Permanent Secretary and Head of the Civil Service, from which followed in 1920 the creation of the unified Administrative Class. The reorganisation set up three Controllers of Finance, Supply Services, and Establishments who were given Permanent Secretary status and were to be directly responsible to Ministers, and were expected to carry on in practically the same way as Permanent Secretaries in other

[11] In my lay-out in para 71, 'Management' would take (2), (3), (4); 'Public Sector' (5); and 'National Economy & Finance' (6).
[12] Sir Horace Hamilton, 'Sir Warren Fisher and the Public Service'. *Public Administration,* Spring 1951. Pages 10 and 11.

departments. It was only on Warren Fisher's insistence when he arrived at the Treasury that there was an interchangeable staff: the original intention had been to keep them entirely separate. The Permanent Secretary himself was not expected to concern himself with the work of the sub-departments, except in a general sense.

Warren Fisher did not like the scheme at all. He described it later to the Public Accounts Committee as 'an extremely unwieldy and top-hampered and unsatisfactory arrangement' in which his own position was 'deliciously vague, floating somewhere rather Olympian'; and he abandoned it as soon as he could, a first stage in 1927 and the rest in 1932. Perhaps one result of this detached position was that he tended to develop his position as adviser across the whole field of public affairs to Prime Ministers, leading in Sir James Grigg's phrase[13] to his 'beginning to look upon himself as enjoying something of the status of a Minister without Portfolio'. A federal structure need not work out like this; but it is clear that what happens at the very top is difficult to judge in advance and without knowing the personality involved. It is obvious, however, that the greater the independence of the sub-departments, the more nebulous becomes the position of the Permanent Secretary.

The most difficult aspect of the federation idea, however, is the ministerial. However strongly supported he was by his ministerial team, the load on the Chancellor of the Exchequer with in effect five departments to run (three sub-departments plus the two Revenue Departments) would be formidably heavy. In the period from November 1947, when Sir Stafford Cripps became Chancellor bringing with him his functions and powers as Minister of Economic Affairs, to the creation of the Department for Economic Affairs in October 1964, when the Treasury covered this whole area (except for some new things since), there were as many as eight Chancellors in 17 years: the overload on the Chancellor was undoubtedly a contributory factor to this, and it was undoubtedly a relevant factor in our economic and financial performance.

Moreover, with an overloaded Chancellor, much of the department's business suffered from having too little of his attention, notably, of course, the civil service and Whitehall management side of the work. The changes in machinery since 1964, whatever their merits or demerits, have brought the load on the Chancellor back to reasonable proportions; and I do not believe that this should or will be allowed to grow again to what it was ten years ago.

To make the concept of a federal department covering all the centre acceptable and manageable, therefore, some arrangement would have to be made to spread the ministerial responsibility so that the effective load on the Chancellor of the Exchequer was not substantially greater

[13] P J Grigg. *Prejudice and Judgment.* Page 52.

than it is now. If such an arrangement could be made, it would no doubt also offset another objection, viz. the unwillingness to leave all the central functions in the hands of a department derived from the Treasury. The fear (i) that the Treasury's attitude will always be dominated by an overriding belief in deflation or economy or whatever the phrase may be, and (ii) that the Treasury usually succeeds in getting what it wants, would be difficult to demonstrate on the basis of the experience of the last 25 years ; but it still exists, and if the intention were to build a powerful federal department in the centre, this consideration and the load upon the Chancellor of the Exchequer would clearly have to be taken into account.

Central Management and National Economy Departments

Another line of approach would be to divide the centre into two (plus the Cabinet secretariat), setting up a new department which would bring together all the central review and control functions, broadly speaking the present Civil Service Department, the Public Sector Divisions of the Treasury, and the CPRS—call it the Central Management Department (CMD) ; together with a new department in charge of economic and financial policy, the National Economy & Finance Department (NEF), consisting of those divisions of the Treasury, and closely linked with the Revenue Departments.

This approach assumes that the management of the process of government and the civil service, the review and analysis of departments' policies and programmes, the allocation of resources, the implementation of these allocations, and the relation between the centre and the departments are different from economic and financial and fiscal policy, just as they are from defence policy or foreign policy or industrial policy or social policy ; and that here is the natural line which divides the centre. There is a problem in this concept, in that public expenditure is a major element in economic and financial policy : but on the other hand, the consideration and decision-making on public expenditure extends much more widely than economic and financial policy ; and the control of departments' expenditure is an integral part of the management of central government. This is a dilemma to be resolved.

If we could overcome the public expenditure dilemma, however, and were able to set up a powerful Central Management Department, together with a National Economy & Finance Department and the nine or ten giant and large departments, we would certainly be moving towards a much more effective and articulated apparatus for running the government's business. In terms of the relative weight at the centre and the periphery, this central organisation would be not nearly as preponderant as was the Treasury in the period from 1947 to 1964 ; and it would, of course, completely meet the fears on the other side that the centre was likely to become too weak once the 'giant' departments had found their feet. In my opinion, this combination would bring us much nearer to what one might call a balance of forces in the departmental system than we have seen for a very long time, perhaps even since before World War I.

The Central Management Department

I see no difficulty in the organisation or management of this new department. One can imagine a number of possible structures; but the relevant point at this stage is that it could certainly be done under one head. It would not repeat the situation of the Treasury in 1945 to 1956, with a single overloaded head, or in 1956 to 1968, with the awkwardness of a department with two joint heads. The Permanent Secretary would be Head of the Civil Service; and there would no doubt be two Second Permanent Secretaries and a scientist/economist of equivalent rank.

One side of the department's work could be described in shorthand as PAR-PESC review, allocation and implementation, both in economic resources and civil service manpower; and the other would be the management and organisation of departments, the provision of services, and the management of the civil service. This is considerable width, but only in the sense that all central work must cover the entire field of government; and not in the sense of width of detailed responsibility and parliamentary accountability which I identified as the factor limiting the size of the giant department. There are formidable problems of how to exert a constructive control of the departments; but not in my opinion a serious problem of size as such. It should be possible, indeed, to keep the total strength at Under-Secretary and above down to about 50 :[14] and the whole departmental strength would probably not exceed about 2,500.

The ministerial task could be done only by a top-ranking Minister. Most of his time would be spent in dealing with his colleagues' proposals, a combination of the work of the Chief Secretary to the Treasury and the work done by the present Lord Privy Seal in the Civil Service Department. The Minister would need the continuous support of the Prime Minister, just as the Chancellor of the Exchequer has always needed it; and it would not be entirely unprecedented if some prime ministers played a more active part than others in the work of this department.

Some people might argue that this was a step towards a Prime Minister's Department; but there is no reason why this need be so, provided that

[14] Defence and DTI each 91 ; DOE 84 ; DHSS 52 (all including out-stations) ; MAFF 32 ; MAS 33 ; Scottish Office 31 ; Home Office 25 ; Employment 21 ; DES 20. Annex A.

66

the Minister in charge of the Central Management Department was a political figure in his own right, and provided that he and the Chancellor of the Exchequer could work together reasonably well.

The NEF Department

The idea of a department in charge of economic and financial policy and specialising in this cannot be regarded as original or unusual. The management of the national economy, home and overseas finance and fiscal policy is a huge task on any reckoning. Within the great area of economic policy, other departments are in the lead in some specific subjects—industrial and external commercial policy (DTI), incomes policy (DE), taxation (Inland Revenue and Customs & Excise), public expenditure (according to this concept, Central Management Department), construction industry (DOE), agricultural industry (MAFF) and so on. The NEF Department's main task would be to articulate these together into one coherent national economic policy, and to support it with the monetary and fiscal instruments, and by such other means as the department would have at its disposal.

This concept should be judged in its own right, starting from scratch, and not thinking of it as a truncated Treasury, shorn of the public sector control function. NEF would have an important role in public expenditure, and would no doubt have a division concerned with it, just as the Treasury now has divisions concerned with fiscal policy and industrial and incomes policy, for which other departments have prime responsibility.

In my opinion, NEF would be strong. Its views about the future course of the economy and the need for national action would probably be more readily accepted than the Treasury's are, for these views would not be seen as shots in a campaign by the same Minister to cut defence or social services or whatever the current target might be. Indeed, it might be possible for those who are responsible for the forecasting and diagnosis of the needs of the economic situation and for its presentation to Ministers to be given a more independent and pro-fessional status, perhaps more like the position of the Chiefs of Staff on technical defence matters, which are certainly not matters requiring greater professional specialisation.

The general scale of the department would be about one-third less than the present Treasury, and the number of senior staff would be roughly equivalent to those of the Home Office or the Department of Employment. This would leave more freedom of manoeuvre to bring in more economic work. It would be necessary to consider, for example, whether the responsibility for incomes policy should be moved back from the Department of Employment, the Chancellor being no longer responsible for public service pay as such, this being part of the Central

67

Management Department's functions. There would no doubt be discussion of the relationship with the Inland Revenue and Customs & Excise, and whether there could be closer working on policy without prejudicing the integrity of the tax machinery. The department would be the natural centre for the co-ordination of mixed home/overseas economic policy, notably the formation of the entire range of economic policies, from sterling to monopolies to taxation to regional planning, which will have to be undertaken as we come closer to joining the European Economic Community.

The NEF Department might still be called the Treasury, and its Minister might still be the Chancellor of the Exchequer; but in my opinion a department formed to be responsible for economic, financial and fiscal policy and for the central co-ordination of these policies with other departments in the field (and nothing else), needs to be thought about in different terms from those in which those of us who have had 20 years or more in the Treasury have customarily thought about the Treasury; for this was essentially a concept of a department both responsible for economic policy and for the central management of the departments. The issue that would have to be considered would be whether this narrower concept might not permit a stronger and more effective handling of economic policy.

Public Expenditure

The idea of having one department dealing with central management and control and the other dealing with economic and financial policy depends upon the inclusion of the review and control of expenditure programmes and policies in the former, and the exclusion of this responsibility from the latter. The NEF would be greatly concerned with public expenditure, as with all parts of the national economy; and would be very close to the CM Department in this field, but CM would have the responsibility.

After ten years' effort after the Plowden Report to handle public expenditure always in relation to the future economic resources and the future taxable capacity, it would certainly at first sight seem odd to divide the departmental responsibility for the two sides of the account. The same Minister, it can very well be argued, should be responsible for both sides of PESC and both sides of the annual budget. It seems to me, however, that in the handling of the aggregates of public expenditure, which is what is particularly relevant to the NEF economic forecasting and to the taxation decisions in the budget, there can be a straightforward operation that fully carries out the Plowden concepts.

The first crucial decision in the PAR(O)–PESC(O) cycle, and the one of particular importance to NEF, is the decision for the five-year PESC period which strikes the balance between public expenditure and taxation—in essence, the decision on the aggregate future public expenditure; which then becomes the starting point for the allocation between departmental programmes. This would be determined from NEF's PAR return (assuming there was one) on taxation objectives and priorities, the NEF's 'medium-term assessment' of the economic prospects (which is where the expenditure is related to the economic resources), and the Chancellor's proposal (as Minister in charge of the national economy) on where the balance should be struck. Of course the NEF people would have been participating in the CM's work on the departments' PAR-PESC returns: and of course the CM people would be participating fully in the production of the NEF papers, just as DTI and DE do now in the Treasury's production of the 'medium-term assessment'. Provided there was the ordinary co-operation between NEF and CM which is common form in this type of work, I see no difficulty here.

At this stage the initiative and responsibility for submitting the crucial papers would be with the Chancellor and NEF, which in my view would be absolutely right. As the process moves to the next stage, the allocation of the aggregate between the programmes, the initiative passes to the CM minister, and this, too, is absolutely right. I cannot see how NEF would benefit, or how the Plowden concepts would be better carried out, if NEF was also responsible for the control and management of public expenditure. Indeed, I would argue that the PAR–PESC operation is so large, that it is right for two ministers to be strongly concerned at the centre, and for one of them to have the initiative at one stage (when the issue is fundamentally the size of the public sector in relation to the prospective size of the resources) and the other to have the initiative at the point when the individual departmental programmes are crucial; and that if the Chancellor can concentrate upon the capability of the economy and the development of a taxation plan, and the CM minister on the problem of the expenditure programmes, the government will operate more effectively than if there were one Minister in charge of both.

I see no difficulty for NEF in injecting into the PESC decision-making their views about the relative merits of the various programmes from the point of view of the national economy, or the considerations which they regard as important for their task of demand management. The difficulty with the latter, as has been public knowledge for ten years, is that action taken in public expenditure for this purpose is often counter-productive, having its impact on demand at the moment when it will exaggerate the fluctuation of demand, instead of compensating for it. However, this is a problem of the business, which is made neither easier nor harder by a change in the machinery of government.

Nor do I see any difficulty in NEF carrying out their normal financial and exchange control business with the operating departments; and in getting their help and giving them advice about the course of the national economy and its problems. The relationship of the operating department with NEF in these fields is just the same as their relationship and need to consult with the FCO on foreign policy questions or with DOE and DTI on the various regional aspects of their policies. This normal interdepartmental work does not raise the questions of control of public expenditure at all.

The more difficult situation to my mind arises in individual policy areas when questions of expenditure, subsidy, taxation, charges and finance have to be taken together. I will list a number of recent illustrations:

   (i)   investment incentives (investment grants, tax allowances);
  (ii)   development area policies (grants, tax reliefs on investment, subsidies on employment, bigger expenditures on infrastructure);
 (iii)   treatment of poverty (social security benefits, tax allowances, exemptions from charges, family income supplement, negative income tax concepts);
 (iv)   housing policy (rates, rents, mortgage interest, tax concessions for home ownership etc.);
  (v)   local authority finances (grants for local authority services, general grants in support of local authorities, control of borrowing, new sources for local authority finance, all related to local government reform);
 (vi)   agricultural industry support (subsidies, price and market guarantees, import levies);
(vii)   nationalised industry policy (control of investment, control of borrowing, hiving off, price policy).

Cases such as these would clearly engage both CM and NEF Departments with the operating department concerned—DTI for (i) and (ii); DHSS for (iii); DOE for (iv) and (v); MAFF for (vi); DTI, DOE and Post Office for (vii). On the general concept, CM would be in the lead in the three-cornered discussion with the department concerned, and this should not in itself present any difficulty. But what is really necessary is to get a meeting of minds between CM and NEF (and the Revenue Departments) on the principles and systems of thought involved in such cases; and this is always easier to get within one department, and this is one of the big arguments for the giant department.

It is relevant that the cases that I have listed are cases of long-term strategy, and in them there should always be enough time to work out the policy in a reasonably measured way; and this is easier across departmental frontiers than the relatively short-term and precisely time-tabled operations. I think it is also true that in the Treasury in the past there has been less of this kind of strategic thinking embracing alternative mixes of expenditure, subsidy, taxation, charges and finance than might now be thought desirable. If it were decided to move along the CM/NEF line of strengthening the centre, it would clearly be necessary to get a built-in system for combined working of the two departments in this field.

This could certainly be done; but there would be an important interface between the departments here, which would have to be continuously watched by top management; and some people might well argue that the existence of this particular interface problem would create a formidable case against the whole CM/NEF concept. It would be a much narrower and less troublesome interface than that between the Treasury and the Department of Economic Affairs in 1964–1969, which covered virtually all the economic and financial business; but this argument could not weigh very heavily on either side.

Conclusion

I do not myself think it is sensible to take the issue of organisation of the centre beyond this at this stage. I have little doubt that within the next few years, if the giant departments go well and if the PAR–PESC system really gets moving, the centre will appear too weak and fragmented; and pressure will develop to strengthen it.

I have suggested here two possible lines of approach, one the creation of a great federation in the centre, and the other the separation into different departments of the responsibility for economic and financial policy on the one hand and management of government and expenditure and manpower and the civil service on the other. As always in machinery of government, there are difficulties in both; and I would not want to see change unless the need for it was shown to be clear and plain.

I personally expect that the case for change will become powerful, particularly as we approach Europe; I think it will be found that the federation idea leads to too large an organisation and too concentrated a load on one Minister; so I would expect the two-department system (plus the Cabinet Office) or something very like it to be the outcome. But the fate of prophets, I fear, in machinery of government as well as in demand management, is not entirely encouraging.

III   Public Economic Sector

In this section, I move on from the structure of departments and the organisation of the centre of government to the mechanism by which the State carries out certain functions outside the direct day-to-day responsibility of Ministers and departments.

Nationalised Industries

I start with the nationalised industries—the publicly owned industries and services of a commercial character. They are listed in Annex 5 with total assets of nearly £14,000 million in 1969–70, and a total labour force of nearly two million. They comprise coal, electricity, gas, posts and telecommunications, iron and steel, airlines, airports, rail transport, and many other transport organisations. The way in which these industries are run, and their relations with the government, are manifestly of first-class importance to industry and to the whole national economy.

In this country (in marked contrast to most countries in the western world) most of these industries have come into public ownership as a result of government decisions based upon a philosophy of government and in conditions of political controversy. For fifty years, since the Labour Party wrote nationalisation into its constitution in 1918, this has been a continuing live political issue. In many instances the acts of nationalisation were carried through without a political clash, and the earlier ones, indeed, by Conservative governments, Central Electricity Generating Board (1926), BBC (1927), London Passenger Transport Board (1933). But the background of political controversy is always there—in 1970 as strongly as in 1950.

Many of these industries are nationalised in other countries, but rarely in circumstances of political controversy. They were sometimes started as State industries (like the German *Reichsbahn*), or had to become State industries in order to make reconstruction possible after wartime devastation, or as the only way out of massive bankruptcies. Without the background of political interest and controversy, these industries in other countries tend to be spared the spotlight that is focussed on them here.

These background considerations are fundamental to the relations between government and nationalised industries. They may get worn down over time, though this has not happened in the last twenty years ; but they will not disappear, and they cannot realistically be ignored.

Frontiers of Nationalised Industries

A natural consequence of this political background is the continuing pressure to change the frontiers of the undertakings. It is obvious that a succession of processes of nationalisation, denationalisation and renationalisation (I don't think we have yet experienced a redenational- isation) can be catastrophic for the efficiency of any industry. The political requirements will always be overriding, but the economic cost of such disturbance must be great ; and one can legitimately ask that successive governments should try to establish situations in the contested areas which will be tolerable to their opponents, and so get some long-term approach to stability.

But apart altogether from party-political considerations, there are serious and difficult business issues. To what extent should the nationalised industry be allowed to extend its frontiers and to enter new industrial fields ? In general, the area of activity of a nationalised industry is defined in its statute, with its position often reinforced by monopoly powers. But the industry will often have taken over a variety of business with its constituent firms. Some may be natural vertical links— supply of raw materials or outlets for products ; some may be naturally related undertakings ; some may have very little to do with the industry at all. Should it retain these and develop them, in competition with private industry ? As the industry and its technology and marketing develop, should the industry be allowed to enter into new fields that appear to be profitable, just as a large private undertaking would ?

The arguments here are not easy to weigh, and they must have a large political content. It is clearly impracticable, and would not make sense, to try to define a statutory frontier, valid for all time, to be changed only by some parliamentary process. The nationalised industry must be able to adjust itself to technological and market change. On the other hand, private industry competing in these peripheral fields may have legitimate complaint if the nationalised industry, supported by govern- ment money and by the profits from the non-competitive parts of its business, is competing too sharply. If the efforts of its top management and its resources of skilled people are diverted to peripheral extensions of the industry's business, this may damage the nationalised industry's effectiveness in carrying out its basic task. A large private business, expanding fast into new fields, can simultaneously abandon others; but the nationalised industry cannot do so. In general, the nationalised industries are too big as management units, rather than too small; and the extension at the periphery may be damaging to the centre.

There is a real problem here, which cannot be sloganised by 'public good, private bad' or vice versa. I am not suggesting here how this should be tackled, though it seems likely that some kind of institutional solution (and possibly mixed public/private undertakings at the periphery) may be called for. What I am concerned to show is that there is a genuine industrial issue, completely separate from the party-political argument.

Organisation of Nationalised Industries

Another kind of problem is that of the organisation of the nationalised industry itself. One of the consequences of the public searchlight upon the industries is a continuous interest in government and in Parliament in their organisation, and a readiness to propose changes in all quarters. This attracts much attention to questions of organisation and structure, which are essentially matters for the higher management; and in many of the industries there has been a remarkable series of changes of structure in the last twenty years, each with its Act of Parliament, swinging from centralisation to decentralisation and back again, in accordance with the current fashion in management doctrine. The disturbance costs of this process, in the successive periods of examination, legislation, waiting for the new appointments, and in getting the new organisation under way are heavy.

These periods of uncertainty aggravate two of the inherent weaknesses of nationalised industry—the lack of a clear and simple objective and criterion for policy decisions (like the role of profit in the private sector) and the problem of exercising effective communication and leadership through these huge and inevitably rambling organisations. To overcome these weaknesses calls for continuous and sustained effort by the top management (and co-operation from the department); and this is frustrated beyond repair if the top management itself is paralysed by uncertainty about the future of the organisation.

It is wise to set up the constitution so that change can easily be made within the organisation, and without legislation;[1] and so avoid situations in which there is general acceptance that the organisation needs to be changed (and therefore a lame-duck administration) and there follow years of thought and waiting for the opportunity to legislate— and meanwhile higher management can do nothing. An industry

[1] Sir Ronald Edwards. *Nationalised Industries: A Commentary.* Stamp Memorial Lecture 1967. Page 7.

which is growing with the national economy (or faster) will need continuous change and adaptation, and a clear strand of management policy from the centre to do it ; if one waits until the structure is top heavy and creaking under its own weight, a revolution is required. In private enterprise the successful firms are those which achieve this continuous transformation. Those who fail are taken over, and somehow in nationalised industry we have to provide for the same processes in a much smoother and more organic manner than is now possible.

The Public Corporation

Nationalisation in this country has been based upon the concept of the public corporation, applied in the earlier cases in the 1920s and the favoured instrument of the Labour Party's programme of the 1930s, developed by Herbert Morrison. The public corporation was to be an independent body, with the board appointed by the Minister, but free from day-to-day control from the Minister or Parliament ; the members chosen on merit and not as representing 'interests'.[2] The statute normally provided for a monopoly, and instructed it to work on business lines, so conducting its affairs that it paid its way taking one year with another. It would raise its finance in the market, like older public boards such as the Port of London Authority, but provision was made for Exchequer guarantee where necessary.

I must mention Herbert Morrison again, for there are few men, either in politics or in administration, who have placed their imprint so firmly on the national economy a generation ahead. I re-read his book *Socialisation and Transport* (1933) which described the creation of the London Passenger Transport Board and his reflections on the whole subject, and I don't know a better practical book on the doctrinal issues, certainly none better for the young man joining a nationalised industry or one of the nationalised industry divisions of the Department of Trade and Industry or the Department of the Environment.

The emphasis was on an independent corporation, conducting the service efficiently and in the public interest. This was the original strand running through the policy, and broadly enacted in the nationalisation measures carried out by the Labour government of 1945–51. There was no great fear about the profitability of these undertakings. There was an underlying belief that the scope for rationalisation and economies of scale in a national monopoly would be large ; that it would be possible to achieve better working relations with the staffs ; and that the undertakings would get their finance more cheaply than private companies could. The concepts were founded on profitable public utilities.

[2] I reject the syndicalist demand of 'the mines for the miners' and presumably 'the dust for the dustmen'. Morrison. *Socialisation and Transport*, page 209.

Government Intervention

But soon another strand began to appear, the possibility provided by public ownership of the nationalised industries, to press them to behave in a way that supported government policy or 'national planning'. This was particularly attractive in the field of wages and prices, but also in the control of investment. When the government were trying to contain the rate of increase of incomes and prices, independent action by the nationalised industries could become highly disruptive, for whatever the constitutional position, everyone thought the nationalised industries were controlled by the government. I always remember Mr Macmillan's sustained attempt, as Chancellor of the Exchequer, in 1956–57, to establish a price 'plateau'. The outcome of the long period of price 'freeze' was that huge price increases became inevitable in July 1957, leading to a Sterling crisis of confidence in September 1957.

In each of these situations it seemed to be common sense for the government to press the nationalised industries to postpone price increases and so check the rise in the cost of living and the pressure for wage increases. But this works straight back on to the Budget; for with the nationalised industry's profit less than it would otherwise be, it has so much less for financing its own investment and has to borrow more from the Exchequer, and so a corresponding tax increase was needed.

At the various public expenditure crises, attempts were made to achieve short-term cuts in the nationalised industries' investment. This rarely made much contribution, for such industries' capital expenditure is not normally susceptible to sudden instructions from the centre to cut expenditure in specific near periods. There was evidence, indeed, noted in the Plowden Report, that this kind of intervention actually accentuated the cyclical swings.[3] The alternative, which would treat the public sector on a basis of strict comparability with what happens in the private sector, would be to reduce the credit available to the industry and to increase its prices.

The experience of twenty years under both Conservative and Labour governments shows a continuing tendency to seek to exercise control of wages, prices and short-term investment decisions. This is contrary to the original doctrine of the public corporation, and strictly speaking inconsistent with a succession of White Papers[4] by successive governments which sought to develop the original doctrine to sharpen the concept of 'the industry paying its way', and to establish ground rules by which the industries should take their medium and long-term investment decisions and handle their pricing policies.

[3] Cmnd 1432, page 10.
[4] Cmnd 1337 of April 1961 and Cmnd 3437 of November 1967.

This conflict of doctrine between the original 'public corporation' concept (as subsequently developed) and the concept of the nationalised industry being an available instrument for government action designed to help in the short-term management of the national economy does appear to be common to Conservative and Labour governments alike. It must, I am afraid, be regarded as a fact of life : the pressures on government to influence the economy with all weapons at their disposal in time of trouble are so clamant that it is hardly reasonable to expect them to refrain from using them. But it is reasonable to try to limit the scope of such interference.

Limits of Interference

The efficiency of the nationalised industries, which, given their size and importance to the national economy must be overriding in all but very special circumstances, cannot be sustained if there is continuous interference from Ministers and departments. There will inevitably be interference sometimes ; but it is very important to get the circumstances and procedures firmly agreed and established. Some of the problems of relationship between departments and nationalised industries are not dissimilar from the problems discussed earlier of the relations between the centre of Whitehall and the departments : certain points must be identified for control, and outside this there should be no government intervention.

In my judgment, there are four areas that are really important :
  (i)   the efficiency of the industry
  (ii)   finance and profitability
  (iii) appointments
  (iv)   long-term development.

In all of these, it is the industry's system and the ground rules that it has to observe which are crucial. Neither a department nor anybody else can do the industry's work for it ; nor in organisations of this size can examination from outside do anything other than check the industry's own system. So this is where to concentrate.

Efficiency. The first step is to discover how the higher management of the industry satisfies itself and measures the efficiency with which the industry works. If the management has an effective system, and reports periodically on what the system shows, there is nothing more that the department can do. The controversial issue is how to define 'efficiency'—the best combination of labour and capital to produce the best service at the lowest cost : if the objective is the cheapest cost, the criteria will be very different from those if the objective were the best service. It is reasonable for the department, representing so to speak both the customers and the shareholders, to approve the parameters. But when the department has laid these down, the operation is the management's. There may be advantage in having a rare but thorough examination from outside. But the relevant point is the internal system.

Finance and profitability. It is now the practice for the department to lay down the average earnings on assets at which the management must aim, and the criteria to be taken into account in taking new investment decisions. When this is done, again, the right course is to leave the management to proceed on this basis. The attempted physical control by the department of the industry's investment, either by fixing an aggregate expenditure figure or by seeking to scrutinise individual projects will be counter-productive : if it does not affect the actual decisions (which will normally be the case) it is a waste of time, and if it does, it is weakening the management's responsibility at the crucial point and so endangering the whole attitude of the industry to finance and the direction of resources.

Appointments. The Minister is responsible for appointing the members of the Board of the industry ; and this is probably the Minister's most exacting duty. Ministers of successive governments have been more successful in this over twenty years than could perhaps have been expected ; and some of the chairmen of the leading boards have been highly successful. But the proportion of chairmen who came from the industry itself has been lower than would have been the case in private industry over such a period ; and the fact that Ministers have so often been compelled to look outside the industry throws some doubt upon the procedures for talent-spotting and career development within some of the industries.

In my opinion, there should be a presumption that the top management posts within each nationalised industry should be filled from within the industry ; and that full-time executive appointments should be made from outside only in very special circumstances.[5] But this cannot be acceptable to Ministers unless they can be satisfied with the industries' arrangements for developing the ability and bringing it to the top ; and in my view Ministers should insist on being so satisfied.

Again, how little basis there is for judging whether a chairman (or an industry) has been successful or not. One cannot judge simply by the industry's earnings, for these will depend partly on the government background and upon the monopoly situation. Nor are the relations between industry and department a better criterion. There are immense amounts of information about performance, but as yet no system of analysis to pick out the successes from the failures in top management. This might be a suitable project for one of the business schools !

[5] It is important to have strong non-executive members of the boards to contribute a wider judgment to their decisions and to strengthen them in resisting the pressures to which they are continuously subjected from every quarter.

Long-term development. The department should periodically consider the industry's corporate plan, and the general pattern of its long-term development (including the extensions of its frontiers). This is the point at which the impact of the industry's plans on other aspects of government policy, e.g. regional policy should be considered—not at tactical moments but when the industry is developing its own strategy.

Wages and prices. On wages, it is impossible for any management to accept the detailed instructions of the government unless the government are in effect willing to take over the wage negotiations themselves, which is the negation of independent management. If there is a national incomes policy, nationalised industry can participate in it on the same basis as private industry. If the government is trying to influence the nationalised industry wage settlements without behaving similarly in the private sector, this is a situation calling for great tact on the government's part. Governments are bound to try to do this from time to time ; but such intervention should be rare and quiet, for management becomes impossible if it is not regarded by the labour force as carrying full responsibility for their pay.

Once it is accepted that the attempt to control and prevent nationalised industries' prices from rising to cover costs must necessarily involve an increased burden on the Exchequer, it is likely that governments will press less hard. The experience of twenty years is decisive, as we have seen above, in seeing the end of such a period of attempted direct action on nationalised industry prices as necessitating such a series of price rises that the last stage may well be worse than the first.

Conclusion. These considerations would seem to set out the kind of relationship between the department and its nationalised industry concentrated on a limited number of key elements—which could survive over a considerable period, provided that the government's inevitable preoccupation with the industry's wage settlements and pricing policies were handled with tact by the government and understanding by the industry.

'Hiving Off'

The characteristic of the nationalised industries is that they are all producing and selling goods or services on a commercial basis. The operations of some are less sharply commercial than others. Some railway services, kept open on social grounds and receiving a subsidy accordingly are clearly non-commercial. The Atomic Energy Authority has combined wholly commercial operations in the manufacture and sale of fuel elements for nuclear power stations—separated from 1st April 1971 into another organisation—with military R & D paid for by the Ministry of Defence and nuclear civil R & D paid for by the Department of Trade and Industry. But in the normal nationalised industry the work is wholly commercial, and the problem is to create pressures and relationships which will make the behaviour of the industry as responsive to market and cost considerations as is practicable.

There has been much discussion of the desirability and practicability of 'hiving off' certain functions from government and establishing separate agencies of a character similar to nationalised industries to do their work. There are in fact very few truly commercial operations within the field of central government, in which goods or services are being produced and sold as the central purpose of the activity, financed by Votes and staffed by civil servants. There are some commercial institutions, such as the Royal Mint and the Forestry Commission, which are financed by Votes and much closer to government than nationalised industries. It may be sensible to set them up as separate agencies, similar to nationalised industries, for the greater degree of financial freedom of manoeuvre and responsiveness to the market. But there are few of these.

The new Civil Aviation Authority recommended by the Edwards Report[6] is a new type of development, for this would be a regulatory authority, and not a commercial one. It would take over the civil aviation regulatory operations of the Department of Trade and Industry (some conducted hitherto by the department direct and some by separate agencies such as the Air Registration Board and the Air Transport Licensing Board) ; and the real interest will lie partly in the Authority's ability to develop its whole series of functions effectively together in this new field, and partly in whether it will be able to take the controversial decisions and make them stick, and so relieve ministers of responsibility for them. If it could succeed in doing this successfully, this would be an important and genuine 'hiving off', for it would be reducing the load on the Minister. But if in the end, the decisions have to be defended by the Minister, not very much is gained.

Services for Government

Another issue in 'hiving off' is whether it is advantageous to put into separate agencies, operating in a quasi-commercial basis, activities of government which consist predominantly of the supply of goods and services to goverment departments, e.g. the Royal Ordnance Factories, HM Dockyards, the former Ministry of Public Building and Works functions in providing accommodation and building for the public service, the Stationery Office, which between them employ directly something of the order of 120,000 people. It would be possible in principle to set these organisations up separately, with their own sources of finance, their own staffs outside the normal civil service procedures, and a top management appointed on nationalised industry

[6] *British Air Transport in the Seventies*. Cmnd 4018, May 1969.

lines, and the outputs sold to government departments at negotiated prices.

The onus must be on those who wish to make the change to establish a *prima facie* case that it will lead to a substantial improvement of the system, well exceeding the inevitable disturbance cost. This should rule out changes of form which are not real changes of substance. If, after a few years, the same people are doing the same operation under different nameplates, the change is not worth making. If the points of criticism in substance can be met within the present framework of organisation, there is to my mind an overriding case against change. To make a major change in order to reduce the apparent number of civil servants (without reducing the expenditure), or to bring about a change of accounting systems which could be done in existing organisations must clearly be wrong.

ROF's and Dockyards. For the ROF's and HM Dockyards, the first and decisive question is whether the Services need to have these government establishments. If so, they cannot be 'hived off' very far, for the Service Department must provide enough work to keep them going, and will therefore not be able to get the benefit of widening the area of competition for its contracts. In such circumstances, the true situation of the establishment will not be changed, and the only question is whether it is practicable within the present framework to make whatever changes in the system of management or accounting practice or flexibility in staff operations are required to improve performance. If on the other hand the Services do not really require permanent establishments of their own, there seems little point in making them into public corporations instead of disposing of them altogether. In short, if the answer is 'Yes', the right thing is to get the best system of management in the widest sense, and if there are old-fashioned civil service and parliamentary practices that prevent this, the right course is to change these practices, and set up proper 'accountable management', rather than to seek to escape them by setting up a new public corporation.

Government Accommodation. The provision of accommodation for the public service costs about £150 million a year for new buildings and furniture, rates on government civil property, rent of premises, maintenance and running expenses of civil accommodation, etc. This is equivalent to about one-eighth of the total cost of departments' staff pay. This is provided as an 'allied service', financed from the Works Department's Votes, and with the Works Department taking the decisions accordingly. The customer department has no financial stake in whether its staff is accommodated in good expensive premises or bad cheap ones, or in whether it gets a new building or extends an existing one, or is in Central London or in Newcastle. When 'last Mintech' was formed in October 1969, it occupied 26 buildings in Central London and seven in the London periphery: we had no responsibility[7] or say in the immense problem of rationalising this accommodation, which was the biggest single management problem in making the merger effective. The Works Department was helpful, but the issue is one of responsibility.

According to currently fashionable management doctrines, the 'allied service' system must be bad, for it separates the consumer of the services from the financial responsibility. The counter-argument, to which great weight was given in the past, is that it saves cost and manpower by avoiding the need for interdepartmental accounting; and that it provides an expert central service. I cannot accept the 'saving' argument, which implies that departments are so wooden that the change of financial responsibility would not improve the decisions or the allocation of resources. I would say that the spending of £150 million a year must justify a very substantial accounting apparatus.

As one proceeds with this argument, however, should departments be required to get their accommodation from the Works Department, or should they be allowed (if they could justify it by the ordinary financial procedures) to build or extend or rent offices themselves? Does the argument about expert central advice apply when the number of departments is reduced to a handful? Could not 'giant' departments look after their own accommodation problems? What is the saving from having one central Works Department for the whole of government?

There is no reasonable doubt that a large building programme for government offices is highly necessary and would be very much cheaper than the present policy of renting; but it may well be much more difficult to get approval for a comprehensive building programme for all departments than to let the individual departments run their own programmes as part of their ordinary budgets.

In my view, 'hiving off' is less important than deciding between:

(i)   single government Works Department and 'allied service' system— i.e. the present;
(ii) single government Works Department and 'repayment' system (? with departments allowed to buy outside);
(iii) large departments each with its own Works organisation (and central co-ordination).

'Hiving off' would be possible in (ii) and impossible in (i) or (iii). My own choice would be between (iii) and a 'hived off' (ii). The argument for centralising expertise would favour the single 'hived-off' body; but

[7] The Works requirements of the research establishments were included in our PESC ration in Category I, so we had some financial link, in the unimportant area from this point of view.

one doubts whether the economies of scale are such that departments like DTI and DOE could not develop ample expertise to do the work themselves. More important may be the development of new techniques and ideas in government office building—with some question whether this would be better done by a single agency under (ii), than by some construction company supplying a market of ten powerful customers under (iii).

The more important question in my mind, applying to all three possibilities, however, is whether the decision-making and accounting procedures, and the control pressures which affect them, enforce (*not* enable) decisions to be taken on a proper economic analysis, relating capital expenditure to current costs over time. This was the lack in the government building system until comparatively recently; and to get it absolutely right, both in the Works Department and in the customer department, is much more important than the 'hiving off' possibility.

Stationery Office. HMSO's work is different again, supplying printing, paper, office supplies and office equipment all on an 'allied service' basis, about £50 million a year. This system separates responsibility from control, and indeed control is very meagre. A department indents on HMSO for its stationery requirements, and these are then supplied: HMSO cannot normally question the department's requirements, and the department is under no pressure to control itself.[8] The position is less complex than in the Works Department; and probably the single department on 'repayment' terms would be appropriate. Consideration of the desirability of a public corporation might start from there. But it is not easy to see in this case how such a change (after the change to 'repayment' basis) would create a big enough improvement of system to justify the disturbance and upset involved.

Management of Social Expenditures

It is sometimes suggested that the 'public corporation' concept could be adopted in other fields of government activity. The advantages which are claimed for public corporations—more professional management, with greater freedom from government and parliamentary pressure— could apply to social services as well as the nationalised industries.

At one time it used to be suggested that if this were done it would permit increased expenditure on these services. Even as little as ten years ago, it was argued that a National Road Corporation would be

[8] In Mintech, we tried to cope with this by conducting 'War on Paper'; pushed by prizes of Premium Bonds for ideas, and designed not only to save paper but also to save time of typists and clerical workers, reduce the amount of space occupied by papers in people's rooms, and speed up the flow of work by checking the flood of paper. We cut personal hoards of papers and files by 30%. But this is a very long-term problem, and it is difficult to make an impact.

able to 'raise loans from the public' and therefore be able to finance a larger programme than was possible in the existing system. Of course, if a National Road Corporation were allowed to charge motorists for the use of the roads, and earned such a large autonomous revenue that it became a commercial organisation, the considerations governing the size of the road programme would be changed very radically. But this course is just as open (or not) to DOE as it would be to a National Road Corporation. The issue is not about the advantage of having a public corporation instead of a government department; it is about whether it would be practicable or acceptable to charge users of the roads on a vastly greater scale than now, and so set up a new economic basis for road-building.

In an 'economy' campaign in the mid-1950s, new legislation was introduced to enable the government to pay grants to local authorities in aid of the cost of servicing loans for water and sewerage projects, instead of giving capital grants to the capital expenditures on these projects. This would reduce the aggregate of government grants to the local authorities in any particular year ; and was thought to be an 'economy'. It was sensible policy to bring the arrangements for the government's subsidisation of local authorities' water and sewage works on to the same basis as the subsidies for building schools, technical colleges, police stations, child welfare clinics and so on. But it was not an 'economy' at all. One cannot get 'economies' in public expenditure by switching from one technique of finance to another ; and the fact that with the PESC system this is now widely recognised is 100% gain.

Whether a public corporation would be better than a government department for running a social service, assuming that the same resources were available in either case, turns on the weight which is attached to the role of parliamentary questioning (or indeed local authority operation). There is plenty of room for argument whether the right units for running social services are national, regional or local ; and at which level the management should be under the control of elected bodies and the criticism of elected representatives.

I would not myself argue that the hospital service or primary and secondary education—to mention two very different services—should be run by public corporations without direct and detailed responsibility to elected representatives. In such services, the requirement of efficiency cannot be regarded as transcending the requirement of contact with the public. Moreover, the expenditures are very large (hospital service £1,250 million, primary and secondary education £1,500 million) ; and the priorities are controversial ; and I find it difficult to give such responsibility to public corporations. We may need different kinds of organisation for these purposes from what we have now ; but I would be reluctant to depart from the idea of direct ministerial control (or regional or local), and close access by elected representatives to such services.

University Costs

The history of university grants may be significant from this point of view. In 1919 the University Grants Committee was set up, under the aegis of the Treasury, to recommend grants in support of the universities. It was a committee of academic people (without administrative responsibilities in universities) under a full-time chairman with a very small staff, whose job it was to make the case to the Treasury for support for the universities, and then to distribute the money. It was (and is) highly independent in its work : it was because of the desirability of this independence (on grounds of academic freedom) that the UGC was made directly responsible to the Treasury.

This system worked very well in the inter-war period and for probably fifteen years after the war. Most informed people in this country and in Europe and America, thought that we had found the right way to provide substantial support of government money for the universities without in any way infringing on their academic freedom and independence. So strongly were these doctrines held, indeed, that the Treasury was able successfully to resist the very reasonable claims of the Comptroller and Auditor General (and the Public Accounts Committee) to examine the way in which these grants had been used.

But as soon as the grants became large, and as soon as political issues began to invade higher education, the system experienced great diffi- culty. When I was first occupied in the Treasury with university grants, towards the end of 1953, the grant was about £26 million a year. In my last year in the Treasury (1965–66), the expenditure was £194 million. Formerly, the purpose of the government money had been to enable the universities to develop on lines that they themselves had chosen. But in the 1950s, the growth of higher education—the need to expand the university population and to start new universities, the need in particular for a huge expansion of scientific and technological university education—became a matter of national policy, not the policy of the universities. The message to the universities became 'what expansion can you accomplish if we give you the money ?' The message from the universities was 'you will want us to do this, and we shall need this amount of money to do it.'

So the grants increased ; the relation between the universities and other areas of higher education, and between both and the whole education budget, became a matter for legitimate controversy. The Treasury could no longer reasonably be the sponsor of the universities and protector of their freedom. The responsibility for them passed to the Department of Education and Science. The C & AG speedily got access to their accounts (and the world did not come to an end). The UGC remained, and works with great effect. It would be difficult to say that the universities' independence has been prejudiced. But the position of the universities is very different from what it was fifteen or twenty years ago—not worse, but not nearly so remote from the government as provider of the money. The combined pressure of the size of the bill (the £194 million of 1965–66 had become £270 million in 1970–71) and the political character of the subject has greatly changed the government and public attitude to it.

The conclusion which I draw is this. The National Health Service and the education service involve an amount of public money several times larger than that of the universities, and proportionately as much bigger in politics, too ; and the experience of the university grants would seem to me to rule out the idea of having public corporations to run them. These are in their essence political matters, in the true sense of 'political', and they cannot be run by people outside government.

Public Boards and Agencies

Another family of public bodies consists of the boards and agencies which are set up to do specific jobs in the economic field, financed from public funds. Within Mintech we had Industrial Reorganisation Corporation, National Research Development Corporation, Shipbuilding Industry Board, Metrication Board, the three Industrial Estates Corporations for England, Scotland and Wales. In each case there was a specific job to be done—to promote the reorganisation and development of industry ; to develop and exploit new inventions ; to carry out the proposals for the reorganisation of the shipbuilding industry following the Geddes Report of 1966 ; to guide and co-ordinate the transition to the metric system ; to own and let and administer the factories set up by the government in the development areas.

In each case a special body was set up to do the work, with a chairman and a board and a permanent staff (normally drawn from relevant fields), separate from the Minister and the department, and not subject to day-to-day questioning in Parliament. Sometimes the task can be done in the department in the ordinary way ; but it is usually easier to bring in outside people both as chairman and board members and for the staff. It is easier to finance such bodies by grants or advances from the department than within the departmental financial system. So whenever a new and self-contained task arises, requiring more flexibility in recruitment and finance than is customary in departmental work, a Board is usually set up. This is normally an economical and efficient way to proceed but I must list some reservations.

This is a good way to handle tasks of limited and relatively short-term (say, less than five years) duration. Such tasks can be lucidly defined. At the first stage an enthusiast can usually be found to take the lead, and a staff can be recruited for an interesting short-term task. But if the task is going to last for a long time, the problem of continuous re-creation of the vitality of the organisation, as the first and second sets of leaders depart, becomes difficult : the problem of careers and permanent employment and pensions for the staff becomes pressing ; and the Board tends to turn into a bureaucracy, doing a good job, but too cosy and too prone to take the course with least trouble.

In government departments, this risk of atrophy is met partly by the continuous change engendered by the flow of political life and public events and partly by the fact that these are large organisations and it is possible to keep people lively by moving them about. In private industry, there is the environment of continuous change. In many of the professions, the process of attrition of interest is well known. But the small public board, with a single task and a small staff, is very vulnerable indeed.

Agencies or Departments

It is the department's responsibility to guard against this tiredness ; and I would advocate a critical review of all such boards after, say, four years and every four years thereafter, to determine whether their work should be drastically reshaped or stopped altogether, or brought back into the department, or merged with that of another body. These are techniques for the short haul and not for the permanent work of government. If there turns out to be a permanent task to be done, of a scale not large enough for a major statutory body with a powerful permanent organisation, it should be done by the department, if necessary with an advisory committee to give it the necessary contact with the specific outside interests involved.

In Mintech we had to prevent duplication between the various Boards and between them and the department. Firms would seek support from IRC, from NRDC and from the department itself. I don't think we ever went wrong, but the problem was always there. To impose constraints upon the agencies which the department has set up, and to require co-ordination procedures will frustrate the department's original purpose. When the Shipbuilding Industry Board was set up, it was intended to be the government's instrument for the rationalisation of the shipbuilding industry : but the problems of Upper Clyde Shipbuilders and of Cammell Laird and Harland and Wolff raised issues far beyond its scope, and the department became heavily involved. Such was the scale and political sensitivity of the issues involved that the government was implicated right up to the neck. But, of course, if the government is going to be so implicated, the objective in setting up the independent agency is destroyed ; and if such a situation is foreseen it may be better to equip the department to do the job from the start.

Departmental Strength

There is a long-term consideration here which cannot be ignored. If the new tasks, and particularly those requiring special expertise, are given to new public boards and agencies, the departments' capability to handle them themselves will clearly disappear. The essence of a good department (and particularly of the 'giant' department) is its ability to handle anything that it is required to do. This involves having at the department's disposal a wide range of experience and strong and varied expertise. If the new and testing jobs (by definition involving its most contemporary State-industry relation) are thought to be unsuitable for the department to handle itself, and to acquire the expertise to do so, a time will soon come when the department will be unable to do so and will have no credibility outside when Ministers need it.

Lastly, one of the most formidable tasks of a department is to be able to make proposals to its Minister for men and women to take on the leadership of these public boards and agencies. A great effort is deployed on this, but nobody has yet been able to develop the technique of identifying the promising and available people in industry and elsewhere and to fit them in to the (literally) hundreds of vacancies that the department has to fill. The success of the enterprises, however, turns on the skill with which this is done. Perhaps a more intensive exploitation of the public service itself in all its forms could help.

Conclusion

My conclusion, therefore, is that the allocation of new tasks to public boards and agencies is not necessarily wise, and is positively dangerous if adopted for long-term tasks ; and in my opinion we have to pay much more attention to our capability within the public service to carry out new current tasks. I think it is right to set up public corporations to do great permanent tasks, and I would be surprised if there was much dissent from the general line of approach which I have described. But I think it is wrong both on the merits of the job and in the interests of the capability of the public service itself, to treat 'hiving off' as a desirable objective in itself, if one means by this the transfer from departmental management to a public corporation or other public board or agency (transfer to the private sector presents different issues). I would myself favour being less eager than we have been in the last decade to set up outside agencies, and in my view we should be increasing our own capability within the service to tackle the current problems of the relationship between industry and the State.

Scientific Research

I could make room, alas, for only a few brief notes on scientific research. I would have liked to have taken the whole sweep of government and science, starting at one end with the universities and scientific and technological education and manpower and the status of engineers and technology in our society; leading through scientific research and the scientific civil service; and winding up with defence, aerospace and the nuclear, and the government's role in advanced technology. During the last seventeen years I have been occupied virtually continuously with one or another aspect of this great spread of public business, and often with all of it at once; and I decided reluctantly that a comprehensive treatment would take too long. In science it is very difficult to distinguish between policy and machinery of government; and it is not easy to say things which are not only proper for a civil servant to say, but which also have intellectual content and meaning, and more than a few days' survival value. So I shall take a narrow segment, and ask some questions about where we are going in government scientific organisation.

Government R & D

First, the arithmetic. The total R & D is about £1,000 million a year, of which the government pays for about half (a little less defence than civil) and industry pays for virtually all the other half. The government's half is also divided about 50 : 50 between work in its own establishments (including AEA and research councils) and work in industry and the universities.[9]

About 90% of the government's share is for defence, civil aerospace, nuclear energy and the contributions of the research councils and universities to fundamental science. The other 10% consists of a variety of supports for research mainly in the industrial[10] and environmental fields. One can argue that government support for advanced technology—guided weapons, Concorde, the fast breeder reactor—is too expensive and speculative for our embattled economy, and that we should stick to less advanced areas and be willing to import the advanced equipments and technologies; or that we are devoting altogether excessive resources to the British contribution to the world's knowledge of fundamental science when we are so weak in applying what we already know. But I will not weigh these arguments today. I am concerned with how the government should carry out whatever effort it decides to make.

Research Councils

The research councils (Science, Medical, Agricultural, Natural Environment)[11] spend about £100 million a year on their own establishments

[9] The source is *Statistics of Science and Technology 1970*.
[10] A great deal of public controversy is conducted under the impression that government research is predominantly in this area.
[11] I am not discussing the Social Science Research Council, which falls into a different economic group.

and on grants to people and universities : and about £55 million a year of the UGC's grants to universities is for R & D. The research councils' money is allocated between councils by a committee of scientists ; and each council is independent in allocating its share ; and the UGC is, of course, independent in distributing its part. The policy is kept as far away as possible from Ministers and departmental officials. The research councils' staff are not technically civil servants (though their situation is virtually the same), and they are not subjected to central manpower control.

There has been a steady and rapid annual expansion over the years of the order of 7 or 8% in real terms : the curve is now being flattened out, but the latest projections in Cmnd 4578 (still under review) show an average increase from 1969–70 to 1974–75 of nearly 5% a year. This is an area which on any reckoning has been very well looked after by successive governments.

The doctrine of research councils follows the celebrated Haldane Report on Machinery of Government in 1918.[12] Beatrice Webb, describing the proceedings of the Committee, records the concessions to 'Haldane's incurable delight in mental mistiness', but she was well content with the ideas.[13] Reading the *Report* for guidance in 1971, one is struck by the total concentration on the needs of industry and the departments : in the 74-paragraph chapter on Research and Information, the word 'university' does not appear, nor is there any mention of 'fundamental' or 'basic' research, or any conflict between these and 'applied' research. The *Report* distinguishes between the intelligence and research work which should be done by departments themselves and the work which should be done in a general research organisation (the prototype of the research council) ; but it emphasised that the relation was 'a problem in correlation rather than in demarcation'. With the general research organisation under the Lord President, he would be 'immune from any suspicion of being biassed by administrative considerations against the application of research'. The purpose of having the general research organisation was to ensure that departments would not suppress research which was politically inconvenient.

The point of having a general research organisation was to provide for cross-fertilisation and multi-disciplinary work which individual departments could not, by definition, do themselves ; and 'the harvest of the results is won for the benefits of the departments as a whole'. Emphasis is placed on the contribution to knowledge, but this is seen as coming 'it may be only in the distant future' from the work on the problems put to the general research organisation by industry and the departments. One gets the basic knowledge, it says, by solving the

[12] *Report of the Machinery of Government Committee*, 1918. Cd. 9230. The relevant section is Chapter IV, pages 22 to 35.
[13] Beatrice Webb, *Diaries 1912–1924*, Pages 137–8.

practical problems—the opposite process from increasing basic knowledge independently and using this to solve practical problems. This is set out very lucidly by Harold Himsworth.[14]

The impression which is left on my own mind is that one cannot cite the Haldane Report either in support or against the present research councils, certainly on the industrial side. Science and the departments have changed too much in fifty years, and have destroyed the context. The only legitimate course is to try to think about the present situation in the same way that the Haldane Committee thought about the situation in the middle of World War I, with the needs of industry and departments first in one's mind, and the contribution to fundamental scientific knowledge flowing from this.

There are still good arguments for keeping the Medical Research Council formally distinct from the Health Departments, with a different source of government money. With a huge nationalised health service, in a field of intimate importance in everyone's life, and great political sensitivity, there is much to be said for having as much diversity as one can.

On the other hand, I can find no valid reason for separating the Agricultural Research Council from the Ministry of Agriculture; for the course of the nation's agricultural development is determined by MAFF through the price guarantee system (and whatever may replace it), and through the services and subsidies which the department provides, and it does not seem rational for the government's agricultural research finance to be directed towards different objectives, or financed from another department's allocation. Likewise, now that we have a Department for the Environment, it seems to me obviously right for the Natural Environment Research Council to be brought within its aegis, and indeed rationalised with the work of the department's own research establishments. In 'Haldane' terms, it is difficult to distinguish between what these departments need (and carry out in their own research establishments) and what Haldane defined as 'intelligence and research work for general use'. As I was expounding earlier, all the scientific work (the department's laboratories and the research council) has to be handled properly in the department, to get the best possible contribution from the scientists, and the standing that the department should have with the scientific community here and overseas. But in 1971 I don't see why there should be difficulty in this.

The Science Research Council covers too wide a field to be treated on its own. I shall come back to this in considering specific areas.

Advanced Technology R & D

In defence, civil aerospace and nuclear R & D (between them about

[14]Sir Harold Himsworth. *The Development and Organisation of Scientific Knowledge.* Heinemann 1970. Chapter 8.

92

£350 million) a major point for consideration is the division between work in the government's establishments and the work contracted to industry. The practice differs. The Army and the Navy do most of their R & D in their own establishments, for much of the design and production is done in the Royal Ordnance Factories. In aerospace, the design and production are wholly done by industry, and the role of the government establishments is to carry out aeronautical research and to work with HQ in monitoring the contracts, providing testing facilities, etc, so that the proportion of R & D done intra-murally is small. In the nuclear, the whole effort was centralised at the start in the Ministry of Supply and then in AEA, with very little initiative in the plant firms' hands.

In the late 1940s and early 1950s it was believed that building new government establishments and expanding old ones was the most effective way to develop the government's scientific work, particularly into the advanced technological fields. In the last few years, opinion (irrespective of party politics) has swung away from this view. If the work is done in government establishments, there is a special task of organisation to make the 'fall-out' available to industry. If the work is done in private industry, then private industry will automatically get the technological 'fall-out' and will inject the commercial orientation ; and the work will increase the firms' research capability and ability to carry out big projects and with it their competitive strength.

Moreover, the experience of the AEA, with the breakneck pace of build-up in the 1950s and early 1960s followed by the painful reduction since, has taught us the vulnerability of the single-purpose establishment. The government establishment with its built-in job security and its inability to embark upon alternative projects without having to obtain agreement (and money) all round the governmental machine, is badly placed to adapt itself to such situations. In nuclear plant, electronics and computers in particular, the United States system seems to have fared better than ours in translating government money for advanced technological projects (defence and civil) into industrial strength. It seems to me unlikely that we shall again set up new government establishments to handle new technologies.

Possible New Groupings

There are now four groups :

(A)   Defence/aerospace : the establishments of the Ministry of Defence and the Ministry of Aviation Supply, now to be brought within one department. Aldermaston has a close affinity to these and is to be brought into the same system. The total staff would then be 35-40,000.

(B)   Industrial/civil nuclear : the reactor and research groups of AEA,[15] and the Department of Trade and Industry establishments (National Physical Laboratory, National Engineering Laboratory, Warren Spring, Safety in Mines Research Establishment, Laboratory of the Government Chemist)—total staff about 15,000.

(C)   Environment/building : the establishments of DOE (Building Research Station, Road Research Laboratory, Water Pollution RL, Hydraulics RS, Fire RS, Forest Products RL)—about 2,200 total staff, or with the Natural Environment Research Council, nearly 3,500.

(D)   Research Councils—Agriculture 1,610, Medical 3,540, Science 2,450, or over 7,500 staff.

The total is over 60,000 staff, of whom about 11,000 are qualified scientists and engineers.[16]

Defence/Aerospace

For (A), which is much the biggest, the establishments' work flows directly from the defence and aerospace programme. The management problem of handling these as one organisation is daunting : the 35–40,000 staff compares with Mintech's total of 23,000 in research establishments. There should be great scope for rationalisation and the closure of a number of establishments, and a huge executive task to accomplish over a five-year period. There will be a difficult top management task of reconciling the large civil aerospace interests of the Royal Aircraft Establishment and the National Gas Turbine Establishment (and the significant civil interests of others, e.g. Royal Radar Establishment) with the predominantly defence interests of the whole undertaking, and also of providing effectively for the transmission of the technological fall-out from all the establishments to industry. But these are among the problems to be solved.

Industrial/Civil Nuclear

For (B), the industrial/civil nuclear group, the position is different. Much of the work flows directly from government requirements. The provision of government support for nuclear reactor R & D projects is in principle similar to government provision of 'launching aid' for civil aircraft projects. Some of the work in the industrial research laboratories, e.g. the standards work in NPL, virtually all the work of the Government Chemist, and much of the safety in mines work at SMRE, is specifically required to carry out governmental responsibilities. Again, some of this is work that would not be done otherwise, but which government wish

[15] The AEA Production Group and Radio-Chemical Centre have now become separate companies ; the main research and reactor Group establishments Harwell, Culham, Winfrith, Dounreay, Risley.
[16] Not large numbers in quantity, though important in quality, in the national total of 240,000 qualified scientists and engineers in 1968.

94

to support as a matter of industrial and scientific policy. Then there is work that the establishments develop for themselves, sometimes in collaboration with industry.

At the time of the Green Paper, *Industrial Research and Development in Government Laboratories*, published by Mintech in January 1970, it was estimated that about two-thirds of the total work of this group might be regarded as government-based—i.e. work that the government would need to have undertaken in support of its own requirements and policies (i.e. analogous to defence work) and which it would therefore probably finance, either by giving grants to the establishments or by placing contracts with them.

The Green Paper proposed to bring nearly all these establishments together (and also the National Research Development Corporation, NRDC) into a British Research and Development Corporation (BRDC) which would be outside the government's direct responsibility, financed partly by a general grant from the government and partly by specific government contracts and the rest from the sale of services, royalty income, joint ventures and other contract work from industry.[17] The size and health of the organisation was intended to depend upon its ability to provide economically and commercially for industry's needs; and it was an attempt to introduce a market test into predominantly government-financed research establishments.

Where do we move next? I am sure it will not be practicable to limit the operations of government-financed establishments to work specifically of interest to government departments. I am equally sure that we should not allow them to undertake substantial amounts of fundamental work which would normally be done by universities. Government industrial research laboratories must be close to industry, and work jointly with industry. The idea of having a public research body (i.e. BRDC) with (i) government paying specifically for the work that it wants, and (ii) government giving a general grant, fixed for some years ahead, to enable the Corporation to develop general industrial and nuclear research of a kind that others could not be expected to do, and (iii) the organisation required to earn the rest of its money or cut down its size has attractions whatever one's political situation.

Many things must be done first. The government will need to work out the future principles of government support for civil nuclear R & D by discussion with the Atomic Energy Authority and the electricity supply industry and the nuclear plant industry. When we consider the future of nuclear research at Harwell and Culham, we cannot ignore

17 According to the estimates on p 82 this would ultimately need to cover about one-third of BRDC's total expenditure. This was criticised as being impracticably high, but this view underestimated the present scale of private sector transactions. The concept was that if BRDC could not sell its services, its scale of operation would have to be cut down.

the Science Research Council's work at Rutherford and Daresbury. No sensible system can have different regimes for these two sets of establishments. Some units, like the Government Chemist, are engaged on government work virtually 100%, and would not gain from being part of a wider grouping. I would like to see a link between the new research body and the industrial research associations—a large number of institutions which employ about 7,000 people (nearly 2,000 qualified scientists and engineers), with an average of 25% of their expenditure covered by government grants. For some industries, parts of the government laboratories might be added to the relevant research association, as proposed by the Rochdale Committee for shipping and shipbuilding.

The question in my mind is whether, after sorting out and preparation as described above, the way might become clear in time for bringing together some of the SRC establishments (the SRC grant-giving function is much nearer the university end of the spectrum), the AEA and industrial research establishments, some research associations, perhaps NRDC : embracing (if one may use the terms in this way for illustration) government-financed scientific research, government-financed industrial research, industry-financed industrial research. By then ten years will have elapsed since the Trend Report (1963). Could the time by then be ripe for lowering the fences between 'science' and 'technology' and 'government finance' and 'industry finance', using the industrial exploitation end to lead the pure scientific work on the Haldane principle ?

Is it possible to think of the work of such an industrial research institution as being financed from three sources—a general grant from government covering the general scientific, industrial and nuclear research, subscriptions from industry analogous to those that it now gives to industrial research associations, and a third area in which the institution itself was performing services and undertaking specific jobs on contract to the government and to industry ? The future of the institution would depend upon the success of the contract part, as it should ; but the sector generating a reliable income would be wider ; there would be a more closely integrated government-industry relationship, and the removal of a number of barriers would open doors to rationalisation. We have not yet reached even the beginnings of stability here ; and we should not proceed to new major reorganisation until the objectives and the potentialities of the various bits have been sorted out. But when this has been done, we should be aiming at convergence of science and technology, and of government and industry rather than build new walls between them.

Environment/building

For (C), the environment/building sector, the immediate problem is to bring together the units now within the Department of the Environment.

The National Environment Research Council should clearly be included too, completing a group of research establishments employing over 3,500 people. The work is a mixture of industrial, scientific and governmental requiring a considerable degree of independence, for this is one of the subjects on which government laboratories have an important role in keeping impartial facts before the public, and in giving independent advice to firms and consultants.

These together with the Agricultural Research Council and the departmental agricultural and fisheries establishments (including the Torry Research Station), and the Medical Research Council and work by the Health Department, complete the list of intra-mural governmental work.

The Future Pattern

We have been through a decade of great uncertainty about the future structure of government research ; and it must soon be resolved. I hope the distinctions between government-financed bodies 'inside' and 'outside' the civil service will narrow and indeed vanish altogether ; as I am sure they would if the parliamentary and civil service rules permitted the same management arrangements 'inside' and 'outside'. We should at least maintain interchangeability and close scientific contact within each of the groups, together with career development and training. I would hope it would become possible to get better interchange between the government-financed establishments and the private sector, but that is more difficult.

The next period will call for considerable rationalisation, not necessarily to create more large units, but to clear up scientific enclaves where small numbers work in cosy conditions together year after year. It will call also for continuous adaptation to the demand for the research facilities (and in some sense the requirements of the 'market' in government and outside) rather than with seeking to find uses for the facilities which are now in being. New demands should be met not by expansion of favoured establishments, but by contracts being placed in under-employed establishments (if such there be) and outside.[18] The proposed division into three groups—defence/aerospace, industrial/civil nuclear and environmental/building—should help in achieving this by working towards multi-disciplinary units with powerful management structures.

I would thus envisage consolidation of the government-financed establishments into groups, in the interests predominantly of rationalisation, career development, and suppression of parochialism and excessive specialisation, with, at any rate the strategic decisions cutting across the time-honoured divisions of 'inside' and 'outside' the civil service,

[18] It is particularly important to break down what everyone in the business regards as a natural law, which is that no piece of work should ever be put in anybody else's research establishment.

8

with those 'inside' getting management arrangements more akin to those 'outside', and those 'outside' becoming more responsive to the policy requirements from the 'inside'. It is still too early to predict whether the organisation will develop along these lines. But I see no reason either on organisational grounds or on party-political grounds why the development should not be in this direction.

IV Conclusions for the Civil Service

In this last section it may be most useful for me to sum up the implications of these ideas for the civil service. I would have liked to have done a substantial piece on the whole sweep of higher education, science and technology. I have said virtually nothing about local and regional government, and nothing about Parliament, which is perhaps the most important of all. I have said nothing about the organisation of relations between government and industry, or about the creation of economic policy; and I have treated the machinery of government as if we were an island cut off from the rest of the world by an impenetrable fog, although international work has occupied an exacting 40% of my civil service career. All this illustrates how immense is the canvas of machinery of government—and when one has finished machinery of government one should then start on the substance of government.

Given the trends which I have been describing, I am sure we shall need a civil service which can act with at least as much authority and responsibility, probably over a wider field, and with a greater emphasis on management than in the past. One of the most important questions about 'giant' departments is the ability of the civil service to breed people who can run them with the necessary combination of management ability, ability to handle policy and objectives and resource allocation over a wide field, and the ability to hold the confidence of Ministers and be the interface between them and the department. Here in the long term is where the success of the concept of 'giant' departments is at stake; and this presents something of a challenge.

Ministers and Officials

Again, if the Cabinet is to spend more time on policy and objectives and priorities, and less time on technical detail (whether diplomatic or economic or military or social), more of the detailed decision-making will have to be done by departmental Ministers and their departments; and the departmental Ministers themselves will require to delegate more within their departments. We should ignore the old saw about Ministers being concerned with policy and officials with administration. It is officials' business to advise their Ministers on policy; and he would be a poor Minister who did not concern himself with the administration of his department, for this is what makes policy effective.

One might see the total work of a department as a spectrum, at one end of which is the formulation of objectives and priorities (which is the responsibility of the Minister) and at the other end what might be called the permanent foundation of the administrative structure (which is normally left to the Permanent Secretary). Near one end of the spectrum, in the decisions how to carry out the Minister's objectives, the officials will be heavily involved: near the other end, in the determination of senior appointments or the working system of the department it would be unwise for the Minister not to be involved. These relations are never black and white[1]; and they reflect the personalities and interests of individual Ministers and officials, with a tacit recognition of fields of prime responsibility.

But if the Cabinet is to devote more systematic effort to the objectives and priorities (and to their exposition to the public) then it is likely that the spectrum will shift a little, and the responsibilities of top officials will tend to grow. It is this kind of consideration, coupled with the work of the giant departments, that led me to say that the civil service would need to be equipped for more authority and responsibility over a wider field. The job of 'civil servant' will not become easier and will call at all levels for people at least as good as now.

Civil servants : classification

Next, when we talk about 'civil servants' as an entity, what do we mean? There is the celebrated definition by the Tomlin Commission (1929–31), endorsed by the Priestley Commission (1950–55) and the Fulton Committee (1966–68).

'Servants of the Crown, other than holders of political or judicial offices, who are employed in a civil capacity and whose remuneration is paid wholly and directly out of moneys voted by Parliament.'

[1] However, over fifty years they have improved. Note the cases related by Beatrice Webb (*Diaries* 1912–24, February 1917, page 83):
(a) Sir George Askwith, Chief Industrial Commissioner of the Ministry of Labour, when asked by his Minister, Mr Hodge, what his department was doing, sent back a message 'it was not customary to submit business unless the Permanent Secretary considered a ministerial decision necessary'.
(b) Lord Devonport (Food Controller) got so suspicious of his chief official, William Beveridge, that he entered the room in his absence and seized the morning's correspondence, destroying some of it and answering other letters himself.

But unthinkingly to continue the same formula for forty years is not good enough. The civil service is four times as big as it was forty years ago.[2] The public sector has grown immensely, and there are now huge numbers of workers (e.g. in hospitals, research councils and universities) who are paid virtually wholly from public funds but are outside the civil service. There are others who are unquestionably civil servants according to the definition (the 200,000 industrials) but are treated entirely separately from the 500,000 non-industrials. They are excluded from the control of departments' staff numbers and from the statistical aggregates and analyses; and their problems are never considered by the periodic Royal Commissions on the Civil Service.[3]

'Civil servant' is not an occupational classification at all; for the service contains thousands of occupations. Nor is it the industrial classification of 'national government service', for this covers fewer than 600,000 of the 700,000. Nor is it a classification by the employer, like the employees of ICI or the National Westminster Bank: all civil servants are employed by the Crown, in the formal sense of the term, but a great many others are employed by the Crown in the same sense, so that even if this definition had a sharp content in terms of industrial status and relations, it would not define 'civil servants'.

There are several 'civil services', related to each other and overlapping, but from the point of view of practical thought and analysis quite distinct; and some more akin to 'non-civil servants' in the public service than to each other. Contrast for example, the central work of government, focussed on Nos 10 and 11 Downing Street; the headquarters work of the great industrial and regulatory departments; the revenue departments; the running of nation-wide social services, some through local government and some direct; defence; research establishments; etc. Can one find the line distinguishing the 500,000 'non-industrial civil servants' from the total of over four million[4] in the public service (excluding the nationalised industries)?

The class structure of the service has tended to confuse the classification of the work done by the service and its relationship with the work done by the rest of the public service, and I think it has tended to have the same deadening effect on the thought about public service and civil service manpower in all its aspects as the Votes system had on public expenditure before the PESC breakthrough on public expenditure

[2] *Civil Service Statistics 1970*, Table I.
[3] Fulton Report (Cmnd 3638). Appendix A. Page 107, paras 3 and 4, points out that the National Board of Prices and Incomes (Report No. 18, June 1966) had recommended the government to aim to bring about equality of status, and that this objective has been accepted; but the convention of treating the industrials as outside the scope of the committee's work was maintained.
[4] The big numbers are of course teachers, nurses, hospital staffs generally, local government staffs, police, armed forces as well as industrial and non-industrial civil servants. See *Economic Trends,* No. 200, June 1970.

classification. We are led to take insufficient account, for example, of the fact that the public service is much the biggest user of various important kinds of educated and qualified manpower and womanpower : in these large areas, the attempt to fix pay by 'fair comparison with the private sector' is self-defeating ; and the various parts of the public service will go on leapfrogging each other (or be restrained quite arbitrarily) until principles are worked out to govern pay determinations by the public employer.

Some things are treated as separate which are not really separate at all ; and others are treated as the same when they are not really the same at all. We are still far from the conceptual breakthrough to get civil service and public service manpower on to a proper classification for policy purposes. Meanwhile, each of us inside the service or outside, has a different kind of person in mind when talking about 'civil servants' ; and not always the best of his or her kind ; so it is not at all surprising if we do not always talk sense even in the world of 'images' and public relations.

Senior Policy and Management Group

It is probably true that the people of Under-Secretary (or equivalent) and above, who constitute what Fulton called a 'Senior Policy and Management Group' (SPMG) are a more homogeneous group than most of the service. They will now be completely unified on an all-service basis, without distinction of academic background, or department, or generalist or specialist experience—the new open structure of the civil service at the top. They will become more homogeneous as the new organisation develops. There were 657 in the first quarter of 1970—administrators 400 ; economists and statisticians 31 ; legal 58 ; medical 16 ; scientific 67 ; engineers, architects and other works group 44 ; others 41. There are perhaps five times as many who are poised upon the various ladders leading to these posts, and, of course, some will succeed and some fail.

These are the people who are in positions of direct responsibility to Ministers for conducting the State's business and running the government machine. They are responsible for advising Ministers in all kinds of matters with an immense variety of expertise ; they manage the departments and a diversity of institutions. They do different kinds of work. Some are concerned primarily with general policy and continuous advice to Ministers ; some with technical work and advice— scientific, legal, economic ; some with management ; and some with all three. But with few exceptions they share the common strand of direct personal responsibility to their Ministers. None of these can shrug his shoulders and say that it isn't really his business : and this is really what makes them one group.

Fulton: Three Years Later

It was towards this group (and particularly the administrators in it) that most of the criticism in the Fulton Report was directed. Three years after Fulton, I do not intend to return to old controversies; but some points have emerged from my own experience and seem important after the intensive discussions since then.

I think most senior civil servants were bound to take some umbrage at Chapter I and this view was strongly expressed in Parliament.[5] The last three years have shown on the contrary, however, that there was very little in the actual proposals to cause any difficulty to even the most traditionally-minded civil servant of the old Administrative Class. Some were already under way; some were unexceptionable in principle but very difficult in practice—so difficult as to be doubtfully cost-effective: some provided valuable support for new ideas. Apart from a few points which were clearly not doctrinally fundamental, the proposals have been worked forward without encountering any serious civil service difficulty except what is inevitable in the hard grind of turning ideas into realities; and the successive reports of the Joint Committee of the National Whitley Council show impressive progress. There is a certain paradox here; but I will not try to unravel it.

Most people who are familiar with the present situation in the service would, I think, agree that the criticism in Fulton three years ago for insufficient attention to management now looks somewhat threadbare. Maybe Fulton has helped to make it so. It may be true that as late as the 1950s, policy ranked well above management in most Permanent Secretaries' priorities. One could, however, make an impressive list of advances in management techniques in the 1940s and 1950s, beginning with O & M and continuing with automatic data processing, in which the civil service was well to the fore nation-wide; and certainly the emphasis on management in the Plowden Report in 1961, which resulted from two years' dialogue between the Committee and the Permanent Secretaries, fell on receptive ears.

The setting-up in 1962 of the management side of the Treasury under a separate Joint Permanent Secretary and Head of the Civil Service, Sir Laurence Helsby, and Helsby's own contribution in this field gave a further push. This has been carried on by the Civil Service Department; and all this has made a great change over a decade. In my opinion it is certainly not possible now to criticise the higher civil service for insufficient attention to management. Indeed, the pendulum may be swinging too far this way; it is too easy to forget that the forging of the instrument is important, but deciding what the instrument does is crucial.

[5] House of Commons debate 21 November 1968 and House of Lords debate 24 July 1968.

Amateurs and Professionals

Three years later, one certainly would not expect to find support for criticism of 'amateurism' in the higher civil service, for the demand in every walk of life for 'generalists' and 'all-rounders'—people who have broad enough backgrounds and interests to relate together a host of different subjects and to handle many different kinds of things simultaneously—is becoming continuously more insistent. It does not follow from this that the right way to train such people is by starting them off as 'generalists' at the age of 23 and giving them a 'butterfly' experience tasting one flower after another. But this idea is outside my own experience in the service. In 21 years in the Treasury, I had basically four jobs, for nine, two, four and six years respectively. In five years as head of a department, as I said earlier, one of my main objectives has been to keep people in the same jobs for as long as four years if we could. In a rapidly changing civil service—and industry has just the same problem—this is not at all easy to do, though it pays off every time when one can do it.

It is my own opinion, ideed, as one who came into the service relatively late in life, and with experience at Permanent Secretary level both in the Treasury and in charge of quite substantial departments, that the leading characteristic of the service is not its 'amateurism' but its highly developed 'professionalism'. This is not a professionalism in education or agriculture or defence or whatever the subject may be, though the people in the departments are not in my experience noticeably worse informed about their subjects than the people with whom they have to deal, although often more reluctant to express an opinion (again a matter of professionalism, for a civil servant must not allow himself to get out of step with his Minister).

It is a professionalism in government, beginning at the age of 23 and continuing for a lifetime. The proof of the reality of this professionalism is that a man can move more efficiently from a top job in one department to a top job in another, than to move from his job in the department to a job outside the service in the same field. I use the word 'efficiently' quite deliberately. He is better equipped, by his professional life and training, to do the civil service job in a different field than to do a non-civil service job in the same field.

This professionalism has its limitations and weaknesses, just as other professions have theirs. I think it is unfortunate that the remorseless pressure of work and the need to maintain discretion and disinterestedness tend to keep senior civil servants somewhat aloof from the rest of the community—one sees similar characteristics in judges. I think the nature of the work requires and develops a sharp critical faculty, and may indeed overdevelop it, though when the opportunity calls for constructive work, no one likes it better. We all know how our professional political impartiality can lead too readily to a tacit acceptance of whatever

Ministers may want; although the criticism that one hears is often the exact opposite!

If I were looking at the problems of the future of the higher echelons in the civil service, indeed, I would devote more thought to what could be done to diminish the problems arising from our particular professionalism, rather than to seek to create a more thoroughgoing professionalism.

Uniformity and Diversity

Most people would now agree that a considerable effort is needed in all big organisations to get the best practicable diversity at the top. The creation of an all-service 'senior policy and management group' is a great step forward; and the removal of vertical and horizontal class barriers in the service will help too. Some other changes which are being made, on the other hand, may from this point of view be double-edged. The centralisation in the service of promotion at the top, career development, training, can easily become a force making for more uniformity rather than less: this was surely the result in the 1920s and 1930s of the centralisation of the top management of the old Administrative Class in 1920 under Sir Warren Fisher as Head of the Civil Service. The widening of the graduate entry will give a greater variety of intellectual performance but a greater homogeneity of educational background; and may well create more uniformity, not less.

My own impression is that what one might call the social composition of the service at the higher level, which reflects the examination intake in the 1930's, may perhaps be more uniform than in the previous generation. Certainly during the inter-war period the examination became heavily concentrated on day schools and on less fashionable boarding schools. The academic specialisation tended to concentrate on the Arts: in 1905–1914, about 25% of the examination entrants had mathematics or science degrees: in 1925–1932 about 16%: in 1933–1937 about 12%. In 1948–1960 it was about 4%. There is a recovery in 1961–1970 to 10%—maybe the scientists do better in Method II—but this will not affect the trend at the higher levels much before the 1990s.

I mention the figures, not because I think scientists are particularly fitted for civil service work. I do not think they are. Lord Cherwell used to say (as if it proved something conclusive) that the administrative class was full of people who knew that Caesar was earlier than Napoleon, but didn't know why the sky was blue. That never seemed to me a good point. But the really important point to my mind is that we should be attracting people from all disciplines and backgrounds.[6]

6 Note two of the three Joint Permanent Secretaries of the Treasury in World War I (1916–19). Robert Chalmers (1858–1938) took his degree at Oxford in classics (first part) and biology (second), and was an authority on Pali, the language of the canonical texts of the Buddhist scriptures. Thomas Heath (1861–1940) had a first class at Cambridge in classics and was a mathematics wrangler too; and was a world authority appropriately enough in Greek mathematics.

For the same sort of reason, I would want to maintain a steady intake of people at age 30 to 40—people with different kinds of experience, coming into the service as a permanent career. I think it must be true that the service gained from the entry of considerable numbers outside the usual channels both in the years before World War I and in World War II. The latter—I am one myself—are gradually being weeded out. At the end of last year, about one-quarter of the Permanent Secretaries were in this category, but the number is now falling fast.

I think there will be enough forces making for more uniformity at the higher levels in the next twenty years or so to make it desirable, by whatever means one can, to introduce a greater diversity. I don't mean more political appointments; though I think that the experience shows that these can be constructive when properly handled. I mean, rather, to get as much variety as we can in the normal processes of entry and in a freer interchange with other occupations. I think this is difficult to do, so one has to make a big effort to achieve anything significant, and I would favour trying to do this in a more positive way than has been attempted hitherto.

Turnover of Civil Servants

When we consider the civil service as a whole, it is much more difficult to make generalisations, for as I have said there are many different civil services, of varying closeness and remoteness to do the work with Ministers at one extreme and the work with the general public at the other. I have spoken of the professionalism in the particular governmental services—contracts, tax inspectorates, employment exchanges and social security offices and so on. I expect this to be the part of the service in which the improvement of vertical and horizontal mobility, career development and training will yield the greatest results. The professional engineers, scientists, architects, lawyers etc, are, of course, professional both in their special activity and, generally to a smaller extent, in governmental work: their work is more interchangeable with the outside world than is the generalists'.

At the lower levels of the service, the work is more akin to the work in other public service and in the private sector, and this is reflected in the large proportion of temporary staffs and the greater turnover of staffs.[7] The outcome tends to be affected increasingly by considerations of competitive pay and conditions compared with other employers. But weight should be given here and elsewhere to the promotion ladders, to career development and to training; and these are all things that the civil service should do well at, in comparison with the rest of business.

[7] Proportion of temporary staff (1.1.70) and percentage numbers of staff leaving in 1969. Administrative, $3\frac{1}{2}$% and 5%. Executive 3% and $4\frac{1}{2}$%. Clerical 15%, and $12\frac{1}{2}$%. Clerical Assistant 61% and $18\frac{1}{2}$%. Typing 62% and $20\frac{1}{2}$%. Messengerial 44% and 17%. Professional, scientific and technical 28% and $9\frac{1}{2}$%. Total 28% and $11\frac{1}{2}$%. *Civil Service Statistics 1970.* Pages 8 and 10.

Civil Service and Public Service

My last point of all is tentative, but it can be important in the long run. We are now creating new civil service staff structures, a process full of difficulty. This is all within two ring-fences, one round the civil service and the other round the non-industrials in the civil service. These ring-fences were made by history, but if our thought and organisation was not to be confined within them, we could not treat them as being of fundamental significance. The original ring-fence has changed, as the Atomic Energy Authority, the Research Councils, the Post Office left the service. In the last 25 years new government-financed organisations have been set up (e.g. hospitals) also outside the ring-fence. The civil service has its own characteristics, but how far are they genuinely different from the characteristics of other employment financed entirely or virtually entirely by the Exchequer? At one time, civil servants had advantages of security and pensions which people outside the ring-fence lacked. But this is no longer the case; and when the 'hivings-off' have taken place, it is always axiomatic that the position of the civil servants 'hived off' should not be damaged. The non-industrials are still kept entirely separate from the industrials.

For the civil servants and the government machine alike there are three difficulties in this situation. First, the number of 'civil servants' (i.e. non-industrial civil servants) tends to be a significant political figure, so that organisations inside are more sharply limited by numbers than government-financed organisations outside. Secondly, for civil servants the possibilities of career development (and for management the possibilities of economies) are limited by the fact that one cannot move from one side of the ring-fence to the other without great difficulty. Thirdly, for the government as an employer, the splintering of the staffs who are paid 100% by the taxpayer is difficult to defend. It may cost the Exchequer money or save it, but it adds great complexities to a subject which is already complex enough.

The natural course would be to replace the civil service 'ring-fence' by a boundary round a wider range of government-financed organisations, and begin to think in terms of this for a variety of purposes, beginning with statistics and central control of numbers. The pay negotiations would go on in separate chunks, as they have always done within different parts of the civil service. Within parts of the wider field, it might be possible to establish areas in which it was possible to standardise management arrangements and conditions of service so that there could be an effective unity of operation between organisations on both sides of the present ring-fence. So one might gradually move from the concept of a civil service defined as direct employment by government departments to a wider concept of government-financed service, and from there to a wider concept again of public service.

So one would have a situation in which the 'civil service' was a practical defined entity for the minimum of purposes, and would increasingly be regarded as a part (just like any other part, with its own special arrangements where necessary) of a wider entity of 'government-financed service' or 'public service'. In relation to the concept of this lecture, it would help to reduce the element of exclusiveness in the civil service; and in relation to the concept of these lectures as a whole it would make it easier to rearrange and reorganise the various units in the public sector in a constructive way. Indeed, there is some analogy with the advantages of unification of the civil service. The change would certainly concentrate attention upon the problems of public service and not civil service manpower, rather as PESC concentrates attention on public expenditure and not expenditure on Votes. These are difficult changes to make; but I believe that we shall find that the trends that I have been describing throughout these lectures will push us along in this direction.

V   Postscript

The foregoing was given as a series of six lectures from 1 March to 5 April to an audience of civil servants, local authority officials, leaders of nationalised industries, and academics. The conclusion was a week-end seminar at the Civil Service College at Sunningdale on 16/17 April, with an audience of over 40 members under Sir William Armstrong's chairmanship. Four other Permanent Secretaries were present in addition to Sir William Armstrong and myself. The Minister and the Parliamentary Secretary responsible for the Civil Service Department, Lord Jellicoe and Mr Howell, were there and participated in the discussion. The seminar was organised into groups, each of which covered the whole field of the lectures ; and with two plenary sessions the total discussion lasted for more than eight hours.

The purpose of the lectures was to stimulate thought about the implications of the new trends in government, which were described by one of the Permanent Secretaries present as a revolution bringing about radical changes in politics, money, size, communications, civil service, in the way in which the government of the country was managed. There was no intention of establishing new doctrine or determining a new orthodoxy. What was thought to be needed, and indeed what the discussions became, was an exchange of opinions on the way in which the machinery of government was developing, more forward-looking and less inhibited than is normally the practice in discussion between civil servants on day-to-day matters. There was no question, therefore, of seeking to find a consensus of opinion or to establish the sense of the meeting.

It was decided that the most useful form of conclusion was for me to turn the questions over again in my mind after the discussions, and to record my further thoughts as a postscript to the lectures. This also gave an opportunity to take into account the course of events since these lectures were prepared up to the time of writing (end-May 1971).

In doing this, I decided to restrict my comments to the first two out of the four sections into which the lectures have been divided, those dealing with the 'giant' departments and those dealing with the centre of government. There was interesting discussion at the seminar about the relations between government and the nationalised industries, but my impression was that there was considerable agreement with what I had said, both among the representatives of nationalised industry and among the civil servants present at the seminar. This was reinforced by letters from chairmen of nationalised industries who had attended the lectures, and there is nothing more that I can usefully say at this stage.

Giant Departments

The discussion, both at the seminar and in the newspapers, leads me to emphasise that the issue is not one between having large departments and having small departments, but between having a small number of large and powerful departments and a larger number of small departments. It is the difference between, say, nine or ten 'giant' or large departments and twenty or more smaller departments. This must be repeated, for there is an irresistible tendency to conduct an argument about the merits taken in isolation from the real world.

For example, with nine or ten departments, things become practicable that would otherwise be impossible:

(1) a relatively small Cabinet (16 or 17);

(2) a reduction in the need for negotiation between departments, and thus for settlement by the Cabinet, and thus the freeing of the Cabinet to perform its true function which is at present excluded through detailed work arising from disagreements between Ministers;

(3) the possibility of creating a real government policy and strategy through PAR/PESC, which literally cannot be done with a larger number of departments; and likewise the possibility of creating an up-to-date management relationship between the centre and the departments and a radical reshaping of Treasury and Civil Service Department control.

If these objectives are desirable, the need for 'giant' departments follows automatically; or alternatively the possibility of having 'giant' departments opens up new perspectives for the machinery of government at the Cabinet level. This does not mean that it is necessarily right to have a few very large departments rather than a great many smaller ones, but it does mean that the argument cannot be conducted as a simple choice between large departments and small departments outside the whole Whitehall context. It would be easier to bring this whole discus-

110

sion into perspective, however, if corresponding progress were seen to be being made towards the objectives in (2) and (3) above ; for then this basic consideration would be obvious to everybody.

The Problem of Size

There was interesting discussion at the seminar on how the problems of the 'giant' departments could be overcome. Perhaps the most important consideration was about the limits of size. The idea which emerged most clearly was that of coherence and scope. Nobody was disposed to doubt the validity of the Foreign & Commonwealth Office (with the old Ministry of Overseas Development added in a somewhat 'federal' way) or of the Ministry of Defence (even with the new defence procurement agency added to it) : even the Department of Trade and Industry was seen as having a very similar scope to that of the pre-war Board of Trade, the possible uncertain area being both the civil aviation and the aircraft industry elements of aerospace, the most intractable of all machinery-of-government subjects, as the continuous changes of the last twelve years have shown. The Department of the Environment involves newer concepts of what governmental functions should be linked together ; but there is no doubt about the incoherence of separating the responsibility for roads and ports from that for housing and all regional and local government and planning of infrastructure ; and it is natural to link the responsibility for all this public sector investment with that for the State's relations with the construction industry. There may be a less natural coherence between the old Health Department and the old Social Security Department ; and an example of a lack of natural coherence and scope is the Home Office, which is a real conglomerate. The general opinion, however, was that mere size, measured by the numbers of staff or spend, was much less important than the natural coherence and scope of the work of the department.

Regional Government

In the lectures, I gave little consideration to the possibility of reducing the load on Ministers and the burden on departments and their size by transferring responsibility on a massive scale from the central government to new elected regional governments. If the policy and administration of the social services and community planning could be so decentralised, subject only to basic national legislation, this would create an entirely new situation for the business of the Cabinet and of the departments. The central allocation of resources would cease to be carried out in terms of health, education, housing, etc., and would be implemented instead in terms of North-West, Midlands, Scotland, and so on. The priorities between the various services would become a regional government responsibility, and the role of the central government would be only to establish such national standards and groundrules as were necessary, and to allocate the resources between the regions.

This system has attractions for the health and efficiency of the processes of government; but to me the overriding objection is the practical political one, that there is no sign of any public desire or willingness to regard such matters as regional and not national, nor for Ministers or Parliament to be prepared to abandon central responsibility for them and leave them to new regional political authorities. It is possible to imagine this happening for Scotland, but it is impossible to divide England into a small enough number of regional entities, with which the voters could identify their interests and which could be a proper basis for law-making and administration. Differences in the standards and patterns of social services have for the last 25 years been increasingly seen as 'anomalies' rather than as expressions of varying regional situations and political choices; and although there has been great political emphasis upon regional problems, notably in the development areas and in the metropolis, these appear as pressures for central government action to deal with them. Indeed, a change of system towards regional government would almost certainly be resisted by the poorer regions, which would then have less scope for bringing pressure on central government to provide *ad hoc* support. There is no middle course in this area: either there is responsible regional government in the social services or there is not: indeed, if an attempt were made to combine both, this would get the worst of both worlds in its impact both on the load on Ministers and on the processes of public administration.

Second Tier' Ministers

There was general agreement at the seminar that perhaps the major constraint upon the size and efficiency of 'giant' departments is represented by the ability of the top Minister in the department to handle the immense scope of the department's business, to get Ministers at the next lower level who can take a full share of the load, and to work the Ministers and the top officials of the department as an effective team. This is difficult in the earlier stages of 'giant' departments, for the position of the 'second tier' Minister is different from that of any Minister in the past: he has much less final responsibility than that which was formerly carried by a Minister in charge of a department but not in the Cabinet (and often much more difficult and politically sensitive questions to handle); but he has much more final responsibility than Ministers of State have normally had. So a new kind of relationship will need to be developed between the 'second tier' Minister and his top Minister on the one hand, and with the industries, local authorities, etc., in his bailiwick on the other. This must be particularly difficult in the early period of a new government, defining their policies and attitudes across the whole front.

For these very reasons of novelty this part of the problems of the 'giant' department has attracted much public comment, but it will solve itself in the long run as soon as the new progression and career pattern for Ministers becomes established. Indeed, the new system may, from the standpoint of Ministers' careers, be both more flexible and more predictable than the old, for there will be no longer two classes of department, one with the Minister in the Cabinet and the other with the Minister not in the Cabinet, and with the department and its Minister sometimes in one category and sometimes in the other. Provided that the scope of the department is coherent, and provided, of course, that the boundaries of these departments remain reasonably stable, this problem of Ministers should be only an interim one.

Organisation Problems

The problem of organisation of the 'giant' department is a real one ; there may be a tendency to over-elaborate it and make it too self-conscious. In the last ten years the civil service has abandoned its tradition of under-management in response to criticism both from outside and from within ; and whenever this happens in a great organisation it is always necessary to guard against the danger of swinging too far in the other direction ; for once a momentum is created it is very difficult to check. In the light of the discussion at the seminar there seem to be five important aspects to consider. None of these presents truly formidable problems ; and if they are well handled the 'giant' department can work at least as satisfactorily as any other form of governmental organisation, and can thus make possible the wider improvements in the system of government which will depend upon a substantial reduction in the number of departments.

Firstly, the balance between the centre and the periphery. There is always a tendency to over-centralise ; and there should be great reluctance to set up machinery at the centre for 'co-ordination' or for any other function that is not specifically and inevitably central ; or to set up 'general divisions' on the periphery. The essential is to make a clear distinction between central and peripheral functions, and never to allow an organisation to develop which confuses them. It is equally wrong to try to make the 'wings' of the 'giant' department (the roc of the Arabian Nights, no doubt) self-sufficient organisations : if they could be so, it would be difficult to justify the existence of the 'giant' department. The responsibility of the top Minister to his colleagues, to Parliament and to the public brings this out clearly : it emerged strongly from the seminar that the 'giant' department must be organised so as to give early warning to the Minister of the appearance of 'big, hot or odd' issues on the horizon.

Secondly, allocation of financial resources. The creation of the depart-ment's budget, and the PAR and the PESC returns, are indispensable central functions. In the Ministry of Defence, for example, it is the most important function of the department, for the decisions of defence policy are essentially about allocation of resources. DOE's part in public-sector investment is so dominant (housing, roads, local authority investment generally) that it is not unlike the Ministry of Defence in this respect, with the very important reservation that most of the invest-ment in the DOE area is investment by local authorities, and not directly by the department. In DTI, particularly now that civil aircraft projects are within the department's responsibility, there is a most important task of establishing consistent criteria for public investment and expenditure over the whole range of the department's business, from the nationalised power and steel and civil aviation industries to the department's expenditure in private industry. There are many govern-mental functions that do not involve the expenditure of significant resources, but the allocation of resources and the priority between the department's various objectives are always likely to be in the centre of a 'giant' department's work.

Thirdly, staff. The 'giant' department is always likely to need a more formalised system than has been common in the past for dealing with departments' staff problems; but in my opinion the more formalised system has considerable advantages.

Fourthly, communications within the department. This was emphasised in the seminar; and requires to be done more formally than in a smaller department. But here again there is a distinction between the problems of expounding the purpose of a new department and the place of everyone in it and the problems of sustaining the flow of information and ideas when the department is a going concern. At the present time the situation of the 'giants' is still in the former rather than the latter category, and is immensely complicated by the multiplicity of offices in which the 'giant' departments are housed; in two years' time it may look much easier.

Fifthly, the Permanent Secretary. Each of the four tasks above is the direct responsibility of the Permanent Secretary, and they illustrate clearly the territory in which he must move. There is perhaps a false antithesis here between 'management' and 'policy', for it is assuredly the Permanent Secretary's responsibility both to advise the Minister on the policy and strategy of the department, and to create the instrument by which the Minister carries this out. My own view is that the Permanent Secretary must leave the day-to-day policy issues to the Second Permanent Secretaries and the Deputy Secretaries; if he does not do this and tries to do it himself he becomes a very troublesome bottleneck for the Minister and the whole department. But this should

114

not leave him in any sense separated from policy or confined to the role of a general manager. His responsibility to the Minister is both for management and policy. He cannot possibly carry out this responsibility if he insists on operating in every major piece of the department's business personally; but he must keep himself in touch with it (just as the Minister should) and intervene, if necessary, to prevent such cases from being handled in a manner contrary to the department's basic policy and strategy. It is too facile to describe the Permanent Secretary as concentrating on management or on policy. The truth is that he must do both, and each in such a way that enough time is left for the other.

Stability

Lastly, the seminar brought out very forcibly the need for a long period of stability in machinery of government. This question may be put most simply in relation to the fact, which is well tested by experience, that about two years are required to make a new department coherent, and five years to get it working together as one team. Obviously, if the machinery of government is changed before the two years are completed, let alone the five years, the effort which is put in to making the new department is wasted, and far from getting gains one is making losses.

The Centre of Government

The lectures on the future of the centre of government were more speculative than those on the 'giant' departments, for they were intended to show where the present trends of development might lead and the kind of pressure for change that might begin to grow. The discussions in the seminar were therefore less specific, and consequently did not lead to the same sharpening of my own conclusions as had the discussions on the 'giant' departments.

The thinking about the future contained in the lectures gave great weight to the procedures of programme analysis review (PAR) and the formulation of definite government objectives and priorities described in the October White Paper. It has from the start been agreed that this could be introduced only gradually, and at the time of writing only the first experimental moves are in progress. In some people's thinking, the effect of this is likely to be greater on the policy formation of the individual departments than on the procedures of the government at the centre : others think that the ever-changing pressures of democratic life will always require governments to keep their options open to a greater extent than is in fact efficient for the management of the public sector.

At this initial stage, different people are bound to have different opinions about where PAR will have reached in two or three years' time. I would not myself wish to change anything that I have said about this in the lectures; for I believe this to be a natural consequence of PESC, and absolutely necessary for the efficient operation of government in a country in which the State plays anything like its present role in the national economy. In particular, I do not believe that the taxation problem can be solved—probably the most important single problem for the future of the economy—except by the route of having explicit long-term priorities and objectives for taxation and for the development of public services which is the essence of PAR. But all major changes in politics and administration require tenacious continuing effort over the years, and to achieve this will call for great persistence at the centre of government.

The Centre and the Departments

There was no disposition in the seminar to question the contention in the lectures that as the 'giant' departments became effectively organised, changes were likely to take place in their relationships with the Treasury and the Civil Service Department, and that these changes would not be confined to the 'giant' departments but would certainly cover all the departments of importance in PAR and PESC. The suggested changes could in my opinion take place quite quickly; and the main obstacle is the inertia which attaches to all systems, the operators of which acquire an expertise that they are unwilling to see abandoned. The point that must be emphasised here is that the change to be made is not one of greater independence of the departments from the centre, but one of creating a proper distribution of responsibility and differentiation of function between the departments and the centre. There is some analogy here with the problem in the 'giant' department of getting the right balance between the centre and the periphery.

Increasing weight is given to setting up accountable management units, although the experience of the existing accountable management units in the civil service (e.g. the Stationery Office) does not suggest that this represents a difference of kind in the working of civil service administration. My own opinion is that the reform of parliamentary control of expenditure is more important and urgent, not because the present system is in general unduly troublesome for the departments, but because the nature of the pressures which are set up in the departments by the system of parliamentary control tends to make it more difficult to bring about the right kind of reforms in the management of public expenditure. Here again, it is not a question of the extent of parliamentary control of the expenditure of the government, but of whether the system of parliamentary control bears on the relevant points from Parliament's own point of view.

Organisation of the Centre

There was a great deal of discussion about the various possible changes that might be made in the organisation of the central departments. There were some who considered that the best course was to set up what had been described in the lectures as a 'central management department' bringing together in effect the public sector part of the Treasury and the Civil Service Department, leaving a 'national economy and finance department' concentrating upon the management of the economy and dealing with taxation. There were others who thought that the separation of control of public expenditure from the responsibility for taxation would create more problems than would be solved. In my opinion, it is still too early to try to form a judgment on this : I think it is likely that there will be pressure for a reorganisation of the centre, for the 'giant' departments will not be content to deal with three separate bodies—the Treasury, the Civil Service Department and the Central Policy Review Staff ; and if these three bodies are pulling in different directions this will be a critical weakening of the centre. But this is all a fair distance ahead, and it is premature at the present time to try to decide what the ultimate answer will be. There were no considerations put forward at the seminar that seemed to me to call for a restatement of the considerations which were set out in the lectures ; except perhaps for the inevitable one in all discussions of machinery of government that in the actual circumstances of the time, two or three years ahead, other possibilities might well exist, depending on changes in the political situation.

Conclusions

This series of lectures and the seminar, in which not only senior civil servants but others from all parts of the public sector and academic life have participated, was, of course, a unique occasion, and it has been a tremendous honour to me at the end of my career in the public service to have been allowed to play this central role in it. My own view is that it has served a useful purpose in clarifying thought about the problems and possibilities of the 'giant' departments and in indicating some of the implications of this and of the development of PAR and PESC and the long-term formulation of government policy ; and I hope the discussions of the State and nationalised industry, 'hiving-off' and scientific research have been of practical value. I very much regret that I had to leave so many important questions untouched. In particular, I am very conscious that our entry into the European Economic Community, which at the moment of writing looks very likely, would introduce a new dimension into the whole subject of machinery of government, and could in five years' time call for different kinds of solutions to many of this country's present problems of government and administration. But this is a matter to be thought about in the future, and it would not surprise me if in a few years some of the pre-occupations in this series of lectures and discussions will appear to have been a little parochial, although the improvement of the government's system of decision-making and policy formulation is likely to become increasingly important in the future whether we are inside or outside the European Economic Community.

ANNEX 1

NUMBER OF MINISTERS AND STAFF
(1st January 1971)

	Ministers	Parly Secs	Staff ('000) Non industrial	Industrial
Foreign & Commonwealth Office (including Overseas Dev.)	4	3	12.8	0.3
Defence	2	3	112.8	143.0
Trade & Industry.. ..	3	2	24.8	1.8
Environment	4	4	38.9	32.9
Health & Social Security	2	2	71.6	0.2
Home Office	3	1	21.5	4.2
Education & Science ..	2	2	3.1	—
Employment	2	1	30.6	1.2
Agriculture, Fisheries, Food	1	1	14.9	1.1
Scottish Office	2	3	8.4	1.0
Aviation Supply	1	1	17.1	11.2
Cabinet Office	—	—	0.6	—
Civil Service Department	1	1	2.2	0.1
Treasury	4	—	1.0	—
Inland Revenue	—	—	69.6	—
Customs & Excise ..	—	—	18.1	—

[Technology (April '70) 4   3   25.6   12.3]

Notes on Ministers: Prime Minister, Lord Chancellor, Lord President, Secretary of State for Wales not included. Mr Rippon included in FCO. Lord Eccles included in DES. Mr Chataway, Mr Pym, Mr Gibson-Watt, Lord Drumalbyn, the Law Officers, and the Whips not included. Mr Howell included in both CSD and DE.

Notes on Staff: Locally-engaged staff (overseas) and military staff not included. DES does not include museums or UGC. Total covers 448,000 out of total of 500,000 non-industrials and 197,000 out of 203,000 industrials.

ANNEX 2

NUMBER OF SENIOR STAFF
(1st January 1971)

	Under-Secs and above (1)	Perm Secs (2)	Dep Sec to Perm Sec (3)	Under-Sec to Dep Sec (4)
Defence	91	4	11	76
Trade & Industry.. ..	91	3	17	71
Environment	84	3	16	65
Health & Social Security	52	2	7	43
Home Office	25	1	5	19
Education & Science ..	20	1	5	14
Employment	21	1	4	16
Agriculture, Fisheries, Food	32	1	5	26
Scottish Office	31	1	4	26
Aviation Supply	33	1	6	26
Cabinet Office	19	3	6	10
Civil Service Department	31	2	6	23
Treasury	32	3	9	20
Inland Revenue	23	1	5	17
Customs & Excise ..	12	1	2	9
Foreign & Commonwealth Office (incl. ambassadors)	192	15	34	143
[Technology (April '70)	85	3	14	68]

Note: Includes all UK-based staffs who have salaries equivalent to Permanent
Secretary, Deputy Secretary, Under-Secretary pre-July 1970 levels; but not staffs
marginally below Under-Secretary level. Staff between Permanent and Deputy
Secretary included in (3) and between Deputy and Under-Secretary in (4). Military
staff; business advisers to CSD and DTI; parliamentary counsel; museums and
UGC not included: no central policy review staff included: RWBC not included in
CSD.

ANNEX 3

*DECISION-TAKING IN THE FOREIGN AND COMMONWEALTH
OFFICE AND THE SUBMISSION OF PAPERS*

A Foreign and Commonwealth Office Departmental Circular
by the Permanent Under-Secretary of State,
then Sir Paul Gore-Booth,
21 October 1968

The Problem

I want in this circular to direct attention to three related problems that have beset
business in both the Foreign and Commonwealth Offices in recent years:

- (i) the drift upwards of the level of decision-taking;
- (ii) stemming from (i), the overburdening of Ministers and senior officials;
- (iii) consequent upon (i) and (ii), a certain devaluation of the jobs of the head of
department and those who work to him or her as assistants, desk officers,
members of registry, personal assistants and departmental secretaries.

Unless we cure these maladies, they will certainly worsen in the new, larger office.

Our external departments have expanded to deal with the increased complexity of
a world in which the number of independent nations and international organisations
has proliferated. With the creation of the Foreign and Commonwealth Office we
are in a still larger and more complex department: and the larger and more complex
an organisation, the higher decisions tend to drift within it. A further cause of this
trend is the pressure on Ministers from the increasingly detailed interest that
Parliament, press and public take in things both important and trivial.

All officers should assume the maximum responsibility and take the largest number
of decisions that they properly and rightly can. Senior officers should encourage
them to do so. (Heads of departments will want to combine this encouragement of
their juniors with guidance on the kinds of decision which each should take and which
should be referred.)

Where Ministers have laid down clear lines of policy, decisions within them should
be possible at the working level.

Obviously the more a problem lies outside, or casts doubt on, established lines
of policy, the closer it will need to come to Ministers. Equally, the greater the chance
that a problem will catch the eye of the public, Parliament or the press, the greater
the need for Ministers to be consulted, or at least to be informed of action that has
been taken. This is an important instinct to develop, and refine. Where the implica-

123

tions are wide, a senior official with wider responsibilities and contacts and greater experience may be better placed to see the problem in perspective than a junior. But the rule is : if you can rightly decide, do so. In general, if common sense and normal practice conflict, then common sense should prevail. (You might as well know the reason for the normal practice in case you have to justify the use of common sense in place of it.)

There are some snags about this :

(a)   you may be wrong ; and
(b)   your judgment may be right but someone above may feel he should have been consulted.

The answer to (a) is that we are all wrong sometimes, but there is no need to make a habit of it. As for (b), I can only ask those whose first impulse is to say 'I should have been consulted' to think again and encourage venturesomeness rather than timidity. Sometimes 'I should have been consulted' means 'I should have been told' : a good 'float' system will often cope with this.

Submissions
Layout

When a problem cannot be resolved by consultation and a formal submission is needed, the submission should follow the order : problem, recommendation, argument, background. This is not the logical order of thought but :

(a)   it may well be the natural order of presentation ('I think we ought to do X because . . .') ;
(b)   it is good mental discipline ;
(c)   it is an incomparable boon to the reader in a hurry. As Ernest Bevin is reported to have said : 'If I have not had time to read the brief, at least I can find out as I cross Downing Street what line you want me to take'. Of course, he reserved his right not to take it.
(d)   The reader has thus been able to see at once what is afoot or what is proposed. If he knows the problem and agrees with the recommendations, that is often all he needs. If not, he can read on.

Submissions should be short or, at the worst, concise. They should be as self-contained as possible : nothing is more irritating than being advised to take the line recommended in Sir J. Snooks's telegram No. 1001, paragraph 17(b). What can reasonably be ignored should be omitted or excised.

An ordinary blue minute should be used to submit information, record a conversation or to comment on a paper where no decision is needed and where use of the above submission layout would be artificial.

Authorship and Signature

A submission that goes up from a department should either be signed by the head of department or pass through him and carry his signature of agreement. (A submission that records a difference of opinion within a department should be extremely rare.) It follows that most submissions will be seen by the head of department in draft, or at the least discussed with him beforehand. Where the head of department agrees with an assistant or desk officer's recommendation and with the greater part of his draft there is no objection to the author signing it, no matter how far it is likely to go up. The contrary convention which has established itself is neither fair nor in accord with the effort to devolve responsibility.

The Route Up

The *normal* route upwards for a submission should be :

From (or via) the head of department ;
an Under-Secretary (Assistant or Deputy, usually with a carbon to the other) ;
Minister ;
and if necessary on to the Secretary of State.

It should be decided and initialled off by the first person on the ladder who can take the decision. (A signature in full indicates that the papers are being submitted upwards ; initials that a decision has been taken and they are to go down again.)

There will be exceptions and variations. When a problem is urgent some of these stages may need to be omitted. When it is more important and difficult than urgent, both the Assistant and Deputy Under-Secretaries, and sometimes the Permanent Under-Secretary, may need to see it. When speed is essential some of the intermediate steps may have to be omitted ; but carbon copies (see below) should always go to those who would normally expect to see the original.

The Permanent Under-Secretary needs to see some other submissions, especially those that bear on problems of primary importance to policy making (as opposed to its execution), the administration of the Service and this Office, or on matters in which he is currently involved or particularly interested. The Under-Secretaries, by attending his morning meetings, will as a rule know which these are. When there is doubt, a carbon copy should be sent to his office.

Prescribing the route ahead

Usually it is enough to give at the head of the submission only the name of the next person on the ladder, particularly if he is likely to be able to decide. But sometimes when a submission must travel far and fast its progress can more easily be expedited— and checked on—if the route is prescribed by the originating department. Departments will often know that a particular senior officer or Minister may wish to see a given submission whether through involvement or interest : a covering ephemeral slip can help to make sure that the submission is not signed off or diverted before it reaches him.

Copies of submissions

The originating department must use its discretion in deciding where to send carbons of submissions, whether upwards or sideways to other departments. A rough guide is to send copies to those senior officers or Ministers who need to know about the submission but may not in fact see the top copy. It may also be useful to send carbon copies in advance to those who may later see the top copy, since this will give them more time to reflect on a problem. It should be the rule rather than the exception to send a copy to the Deputy or Assistant Under-Secretary to whom the submission itself is not sent. In addition it will often be useful for geographical departments to send a copy to a functional (e.g. economic) Under-Secretary, and functional departments to a geographical Under-Secretary. The PUS will often be a recipient, as will the Ministers concerned.

When time does not allow the submission to follow the route which would otherwise be best, copies should clearly be sent to those who should have seen, but had to miss, the top copy. (Here too, ephemeral slips can help.)

Copying should be for a reason, rather than just in case, since the flow of paper must be strictly and genuinely disciplined.

Delegation

Ideally each officer, at whatever level, should be free of those tasks which he can delegate so that he can give his attention to those he cannot. I hope heads of departments will encourage their desk officers, registry staff, personal assistants and departmental secretaries to handle as much ordinary day-to-day business as each can. This should provide registry staffs, personal assistants and secretaries with more interesting work and more responsibility, or, at the very least, greater variety in their jobs.

ANNEX 4

**Heads of the Civil Service; Permanent Secretaries
of the Treasury; Secretaries of the Cabinet
1945 to 1971**

March 1945 to Dec 1946	Sir Edward Bridges, Permanent Secretary of the Treasury and Head of the Civil Service, and Secretary of the Cabinet. [This was announced as 'a temporary measure to meet the special circumstances of the war and the period of the peace settlements.']
1947 to 1956	Sir Edward Bridges, Permanent Secretary of the Treasury and Head of the Civil Service. Sir Norman Brook as Secretary of the Cabinet.
1956 to 1962	Treasury divided into two sides, the economic and financial side and the management side, each under a Joint Permanent Secretary of the Treasury. Sir Norman Brook, Secretary of the Cabinet, became Joint Permanent Secretary of the Treasury (management side), and Head of the Civil Service: Sir Roger Makins (1956–59) and Sir Frank Lee (1960–62), became Joint Permanent Secretary of the Treasury (economic and financial side).
	Reorganisation of Treasury in autumn 1962 left it still with two Joint Permanent Secretaries, and a separate Secretary of the Cabinet. Sir Laurence Helsby became Joint Permanent Secretary of the Treasury (management side) and Head of the Civil Service: Sir William Armstrong became Joint Permanent Secretary of the Treasury (economic and financial side): Sir Burke Trend became Secretary of the Cabinet.
1964 to 1969	Part of the economic and financial side of the Treasury split off in November 1964 and joined with parts of other Departments to form Department of Economic Affairs, whose Permanent Secretaries were Sir Eric Roll (1964–66), Sir Douglas Allen (1966–68) and Sir William Nield (1968 to the end of DEA in October 1969).
1968	Management side of Treasury split off in November 1968 to become Civil Service Department (responsible to the Prime Minister). The situation then was, and still is (June 1971): Sir William Armstrong, Permanent Secretary of the Civil Service Department and Head of the Civil Service (he had in April 1968 moved to Sir Laurence Helsby's post on the latter's retirement): Sir Burke Trend, Secretary of the Cabinet: Sir Douglas Allen, Permanent Secretary of the Treasury.

ANNEX 5

NATIONALISED INDUSTRIES

		Average net assets			Annual fixed investment in UK	
	Employ-ees March 1970 ('000)	Total (£mn.)	per employee (£'000)	Net income as % of assets	Total (£mn.)	per employee (£'000)
Post Office ..	420	2,412	5.8	7.4	463	1.1
National Coal Board	376	697	1.9	1.3	73	0.2
Railways Board	275	1,504	5.6	3.7	89	0.3
British Steel Corporation ..	249	1,168	4.7	2.5	139	0.5
Electricity Council & Boards (inc. Scotland) ..	216	5,465	25.3	6.3	474	2.2
Gas Council & Boards ..	120	1,570	13.1	6.5	209	1.7
National Bus Company	80	101	1.3	7.4	13	0.2
London Transport	69	302	4.4	0.2	13	0.2
Airways Corporations	45	365	8.1	13.0	102	2.3
British Transport Docks Board ..	12	118	9.8	3.6	13	1.1
British Airports Authority ..	4	69	17.2	13.4	11	2.7
British Waterways Board	3	12	4.0	0.8	1	0.3
Other transport ..	85	—	—	—	31	0.4
TOTAL	1,954	13,721	7.0	5.8	1,621	0.8

NOTES
Average net assets and net income refer to financial years of the industries, as near as possible to 1969–70. Investment is average of three years 1969–70 to 1971–72 estimates. London Transport covers period up to transfer to Greater London Council at 1 January 1970. 'Other Transport' consists of National Freight Company, Scottish Transport Group, and Transport Holding Company. Totals not necessarily the sum of individuals because of different dates etc.

Printed in England for Her Majesty's Stationery Office by
Headley Brothers Ltd 109 Kingsway London WC2 and Ashford Kent
Dd. 160144 K24 2/72